# Butter Down the Well

# Butter Down the Well
Reflections of a Canadian Childhood

## Robert Collins

Western Producer Prairie Books,
Saskatoon, Canada

Jacket and book design by Ray Statham / Statham
Design Inc.

Printed and bound in Canada by
Modern Press ~⚡1
Saskatoon, Saskatchewan

Western Producer Prairie Books publications are
produced and manufactured in the middle of
western Canada by a unique publishing venture
owned by a group of prairie farmers who are
members of Saskatchewan Wheat Pool. Our first
book in 1954 was a reprint of a serial originally
carried in *The Western Producer*, a weekly newspaper
serving western Canadian farmers since 1923. We
continue the tradition of providing enjoyable and
informative reading for all Canadians.

Canadian Cataloguing in Publication Data
    Collins, Robert, 1924-
        Butter down the well

        ISBN 0-88833-060-X
        1. Collins, Robert, 1924-
        2. Saskatchewan - History. I. Title.
        FC3523.1.C64A3 971.24'0924 C80-091034-6
        F1072.C64

For my father, mother and brother

# Contents

# Acknowledgments

"The Night the King Came to Moose Jaw" is reprinted with permission. (Copyright © 1973 Reader's Digest Association Canada Ltd.) Scattered snippets from two other *Reader's Digest* articles likewise appear here with permission. I am particularly grateful to *Digest* editors Charles Magill and Charles Smith whose encouragement and suggestions, over five years, persuaded me to complete this work.

Walter Bell, Cora and Irene Lightbody, Gordon Smart, Jean Dempson Hook and my mother, with her photographic memory, all contributed recollections. To them, and to Ian Bickle who helped find a home for the manuscript, my thanks.

# Butter Down the Well

# Prologue

He was such a dear, decent, trouble-prone, mercurial man, my father.

On the days when he was not hurting, racked with kidney pains from the waterlogged trenches of World War I — or in high dudgeon, invoking God's wrath on the Depression, Mackenzie King and all goddam Liberals of federal or provincial persuasion — he was the best of companions.

On those good days, roughly one out of every two, the shaggy, red awnings of his eyebrows shot up over his blue eyes, and his pink, freckled cheeks fell in folds and creases around an impish grin. He joked and teased and sang. His tenor soared like a bugle to the tune of "The Irish Washerwoman":

O, Brian O'Lynn had no britches to wear,
So they gave him a sheepskin to make him a
   pair,

With the woolly side out and the fleshy side in,
"Oh, they scratch like the DIVIL!" said
Brian O'Lynn.

How I loved that crazy Irish tune.
"One-more-time!" I always yelled, just as he knew I
would. "Do-it-one-more-time-hey-please-Daddy?"
So he'd bellow an encore, finishing off with a step
dance that rattled the coal-oil lamps and sent the
dog skittering behind the kitchen stove.

Oh, I could *see* Brian O'Lynn. He was a stubby,
pink-mottled, cartoon-character Irishman with
eyebrows like my father's and a clay pipe and a
green feather in his hat. Always doing things the
wrong way or the hard way — look at those
inside-out pants, rasping and chafing his poor
bedeviled bum! — but always laughing it off. And
wasn't that the way of the world? Just one damn
thing after another, but never let it get you down.
My father said so, and lived it every day.

Something about that song stuck in my head
long after I had grown. It was not *just* a song, but a
dare, a defiant jeer at the Fates that try to drag a
man down. I sang it for my little daughters and
they, too, giggled and shouted for more. Because it
was silly and it rhymed and — well, who could
resist a Brian O'Lynn?

And now, the more the years go by, the better I
know and love the memory of my father-cum-Brian
O'Lynn. He was a rare one. He was a survivor, but
never at the expense of his fellow humans, and no
higher tribute can I pay. He is the hero of this story
— he and a supporting cast of other survivors from
a time long-gone but worth remembering. How
right, how exquisitely appropriate, that all of us
lived in Saskatchewan, the province that was

forever being slapped down by dust storms and the Depression, and was forever stubbornly fighting its way back up again.

It was a hard, happy, simple time that stripped away the superficial wrappings of women and men and let their souls shine through.

# 1

## Spoken For

It is a Sunday afternoon in May 1918. The cocky little Irishman, John Douglas Collins — war veteran, bachelor and proud owner of a ridiculous one-room shack and 320 acres of Saskatchewan sod and rocks — is shaving with particular care. He pats his cheeks with Aqua Velva and slicks down his thinning red locks with Yardley's Brilliantine. He knots a tie around his detachable celluloid collar, pulls on the brown worsted suit and patent leather shoes, tucks a gold pocket watch with a trailing gold chain into his vest, and tilts a soft felt fedora over one eye. Among fellow settlers who favor Mackinaw windbreakers and corduroy caps, he is known as a snappy dresser.

Now he hitches his fast red mare, Patsy, to the buggy and trots four miles cross-country through the greening prairie grass, through the clean springtime smells of life-again, to the farm of his old pal, Cooney Allen. Collins is, in the local vernacular, "going girling."

He has no burning desire to see Cooney this day, and even

*less to see Cooney's wife, Jenny, whose tongue, they say, is sharper than a gopher's thumbnail. Jenny speaks her mind. "Stuck on himself!" she has been telling other wives at the quilting bees and schoolhouse socials. "Never saw a man so stuck on himself as that Jack Collins!" And the others, yearning for gossip as the budding crops thirst for a three-day rain, eagerly nod their marcelled heads over the teacups and the darting needles.*

*So why is Collins venturing into the No Man's Land of Jenny's parlor? For a glimpse of the new "school marm" boarding with the Allens. Just in from North Dakota, she is reported to be a "good looker," which, next to being a good worker, is the highest accolade a woman can earn in these parts.*

*From the moment he lays eyes on Floy Leona Hartzell — glossy chestnut hair, large dark eyes, high cheekbones and sensitive lips that belie the determined set of her chin — he is smitten. After the minimum permissible small talk, he makes his move.*

*"May I see you to church this evening, Miss Hartzell?"*

*Church is the last place he wants to be, but church is the only place a man can take a respectable woman on a southern Saskatchewan Sunday in 1918. He reasons that Miss Hartzell, being of church-going stock, will fall love-struck at his feet.*

*He is dead wrong. Miss Hartzell does, indeed, stem from a long line of nondancing, nondrinking, nonsmoking God-fearing Methodists. But precisely because of this, her eyes now register mild dismay. Is the man mad? They have only just met!*

*"Thank you, Mr. Collins, but I really don't think we have known each other long enough."*

*My father-to-be withdraws prudently, but not for long. Soon he is squiring her to church and to dances, box socials and whist drives. His good manners, education and dress are something of a standout in this time and place. He is only five-foot-nine but broad shouldered, nearly bald but with a finely chiselled profile. He loves to sing and read, as does she. And on days when the memories and ills of the war do not haunt him, his humor is irresistible. It is clear to their neighbors as summer wears on that Miss Hartzell is "spoken for."*

*One night that fall, clattering home in the buggy, he asks her to marry him in two years.*

*"By then," he explains, "I should be strong enough to work again."*

*"Oh yes, Jack!" she says. "Of course I'll wait!" Two years is not long in these unhurried times.*

*An influenza epidemic — the terrible epidemic that sweeps North America — closes her school and sends her home to the United States. He stays on in Saskatchewan, in and out of military hospitals, trying to farm, eking out a living on his disability pension, filling the mails with letters to North Dakota. She keeps all his letters tied with pink ribbon. Their course is set for a lifetime.*

To any who knew them it seemed an unlikely match. They both revered music and learning, and both loathed the thought of ever accepting charity. Beyond that they were as different as fire and water. He leaped from peaks of delight to depths of despair. She ran steady and even, never swerving from her goals. Somehow this peculiar blend produced the strongest possible alloy for marriage.

Such strange and different paths were those that drew them together. Jack Collins, a Belfast boy raised in London, came to the New World in 1912 to seek his fortune. Slim cigar clenched in his teeth, jaunty broad-brimmed hat cocked over one eye, he had no doubt that he would prosper. He apprenticed as an Ontario farmhand and, one snowy day in 1913, homesteaded on a half section of prairie sixty miles southwest of Moose Jaw. He knew nothing about good land or bad.

If only he could have known that, back in the mists of time, the great glaciers came clawing and scrabbling down from the Pole over this place, advancing, receding, building hills and coulees, grinding a rubble of stone into the pores of the soil. If only he had seen it in spring, with rocks emerging like raisins from a pudding, he might have tried for flatter, richer land to the south. The stony, hilly farm would never be fruitful or easy to till.

But it was *his*, which was all that mattered then. The idea of being landowner was beguiling. He was not at all sure he wanted to farm; there'd be time to figure that out. But he had scarcely built his shack and broken sod when the world was at war.

He enlisted instantly in the Lord Strathcona Horse, a cavalry regiment out of Winnipeg — so eager to be accepted that he deliberately subtracted five years from his age, making himself twenty-eight. Two months after war was declared he was on a thirty-eight-ship flotilla bound for England with the first Canadian contingent, a slim, erect figure in olive-drab with lanyard, peaked hat, glistening boots and spurs topped with tight puttees.

He was a loyal but prickly soldier. One day he led a small angry delegation of fellow privates on deck with his dinner ration — a single putrid fish — speared on his bayonet. He thrust it under an officer's nose.

"Here, Sir!" he cried, in the stentorian voice that burst surprisingly from so short a man, "Would *you* eat this?"

"Take it away, take it away!" gasped the officer. Remarkably, Trooper Collins was not tossed in the brig, but he never made Lance-Corporal either, as his mates did. His resentment of officers, indeed of most organized authority, was almost an obsession, and he never bothered to curb his tongue.

The Strathconas spent a muddy, miserable winter camped on Salisbury Plain, training for a mode of warfare already obsolete. In April the Germans loosed poison gas at Ypres. An urgent call went out for more infantrymen. The Strathconas volunteered, leaving their horses behind. Within twelve days, long on courage but short on preparation, those gallant men switched swords and riding crops for lumpy backpacks and dishpan helmets, and crossed the Channel.

Afterward my father remembered only snippets of his months in the trenches. From those fragments, and from the diary of a man who served beside him, comes a glimpse of the horror: water to their waists, lice, mangled corpses, stutter of machine guns, scream of heavy shells, long night marches through quagmire and barbed wire, men dying, men dying, men dying . . . .

He was carried out in September, grossly bloated, probably gassed. After a year in hospitals he was discharged with a 75 percent disability pension, heart and kidney damage, a spot on his lungs and chronic rheumatism.

"No liquor, no smoking, no indoor work," ordered the medical officer. "You *must* live outdoors."

He went back to the farm, although even by 1917 he couldn't walk a hundred yards without losing his breath. When he stepped off the train in Saskatchewan a former neighbor, there to meet him, stared in disbelief: my father was pale and gaunt with the wrinkled face of an old man.

"My God, Jack, what have they done to you!" the neighbor said, and wept.

Most people back home couldn't comprehend the war. It was far far away and there was no radio or television to bring it into their living rooms. To the non-Britons among them it was a foreigners' war. Some farm folk had prospered from it but none could imagine its horror. My father hated to talk about it, but to deny it would render meaningless everything he and the others had suffered for. His short temper flared up in violent arguments.

He was thirty-seven when he met my mother but thought he was thirty-two. (Somehow, in the war's blocking-out of memories, he forgot that he'd diddled his age to enlist.) Yet she at twenty-two was in some ways more mature than he. Persistence, perseverance, Spartan self-denial, were born in her. Her Pennsylvania Dutch ancestors had trekked from New York to Iowa in covered wagons. Some had been in the Civil War, and one had languished in the infamous Andersonville prison. Several, including her mother, were teachers. A distant cousin was the poet Joyce Kilmer ("I think that I shall never see/A poem lovely as a tree . . .").

Her childhood, with ten brothers and sisters, in Iowa and on a North Dakota farm, was all poverty and piety. On week nights, storytelling and games were permitted, but never sinful dancing. Once the young people were singing and skipping to "Skip to My Lou, My Darling." But when a harmonica picked up the tune, the ranking aunt strode grimly from the kitchen and stopped it. Instrumental music turned the game into a dance, she ruled.

Church on Sunday was mandatory. When she was fourteen the family went to a revival meeting. "All those who think they are going to Heaven, stand up!" exhorted the preacher. Every Hartzell did, except Floy Leona. Scrupulously honest as always, she was not *certain* about the hereafter, to her father's chagrin, and refused to speculate.

She won a scholarship but couldn't indulge in university. Instead, after a summer course in teaching, she was in charge of her own classroom, sending back part of the fifty-dollars-a-month salary to help her mother. Once, unbearably homesick, she walked the ten miles home, wearing high-heeled shoes and carrying a suitcase. Her toenails turned black-and-blue. But now, as an adult out on her own, she indulged one secret yearning: she learned to dance — in well-chaperoned halls, where every dance partner was formally introduced.

She married my father on New Year's Eve 1920, in a Presbyterian parsonage. Coming out in a freezing rain, he slipped on the steps. A hundred times over, in after years, he told anyone who would listen that this was "the beginning of my downfall!" She was expected to laugh on this cue and never failed him — in that or anything else.

Back at the farm their first official act, by prairie custom, was to sponsor their own wedding dance. Everyone was welcome from miles around. As a colorful and controversial figure, Jack Collins was certain to draw a crowd.

The bride was terrified. She, her dancing and her cooking would be under the community microscope. She baked twelve cakes and twenty oversize loaves of bread. He sliced a twenty-pound ham. They filled three cartons with sandwiches and brewed four pounds of coffee, black as an engine driver's boot, in a copper wash boiler.

Throngs of settlers shoe-horned themselves into the one-room schoolhouse. Collins' last ten dollars hired the district's best fiddler, a cowboy named Jimmy Dunlop from the nearby W-Bar ranch. Dunlop sawed off three-steps, two-steps, polkas, fox trots and cross-country waltzes. Every man wanted to dance with the bride and thirty or forty did.

Toward dawn the last revellers rattled home in their wagons and buggies, tossing compliments over their shoulders: "Real good 'do,' Jack" and "Liked yer cake, Miz Collins." The worn-out bride and penniless groom had passed muster. Now they had to scrub the schoolhouse floor in return for getting it rent-free.

The honeymoon was over.

# 2

# West of the 3rd Meridian

Eighteen months before the wedding my mother had eyed my father's bachelor shack with ill-disguised disgust. It was a single room with a one-slant roof, a bare-boards parallelogram rising stark and ugly from the grass.

"Jack, I can't live in that — that *thing* !" she said. "I want a proper house."

"Of course you want a proper house, and a proper house you shall have!" he cried extravagantly. "Just draw me a picture of what you'd like."

She sketched a charming one-storey frame building with an attic dormer, a big bay window and a shady east verandah. Like every other prairie person of his time my father then turned to Timothy Eaton's mail-order catalogue for comfort and advice. It was a personal thing, the bond between customers and Mr. Eaton. Although Timothy was already dead a dozen years, my parents and their neighbors invariably addressed him by name: "Well, let's see what Timothy Eaton's got on sale this time."

In 1919 Timothy's main catalogue offered B.C. salmon at 15¢ a tin, bacon at 38¢ a pound, genuine dogskin coats for $34.50 and the ever-popular "Venus de Milo front-lace corset with famous Flex-o-steel boning" at $3.75. His supplementary Soldiers' Settlement catalogue held all the farm machinery a veteran could ever want. Most important, Timothy's Building Supplies catalogue sold *complete* houses: lumber, paint, hardware, nails, the exact amounts needed for each of nearly a dozen house plans. One of them was Modern Home #663, "designed especially for young house-keepers — beginners in matrimony."

What luck! They were beginners in matrimony — and #663 was almost identical to my mother's sketch. Just one problem: the material alone cost $883.81. My father didn't have it. Nor did he have horses, cows, chickens, ploughs, cultivators, hay mower, barn, granaries, any of the hundred-and-one essential bits of farming paraphernalia.

A cautious man would have given up, but not a Brian O'Lynn. He took out a three-thousand-dollar mortgage on his land, although he loathed debt. At a time when the finest tweed suit cost only twelve dollars, three thousand dollars was a crushing burden. He bought the lumber and gave Mother's sketch and the page from Eaton's catalogue to a local handyman. Up went the house. It took him twenty-three years to pay off the mortgage but he begrudged not a penny of it.

He was an incurable romantic. He set the house just so, on a little hill with its face to the sun and its back to the north winds. At thirty feet long by twenty feet wide, it was no bigger than a rich man's recreation room, but he fenced a ten-acre surrounding yard, a grand estate that made up for the modest dimensions within.

By autumn 1920 it was ready, although never to be finished according to plan. Year after year if the crops didn't fail the price of grain did. Spare cash went for human and animal survival. Little luxuries were put off until "next year." Next year never came.

The house was painted just once, white with green trim. Soon the wind and rain and snow buffed and scoured it to silver gray. Indoors, the plan for plastered walls gave way to heavy paper pasted over boards and tinted with calcimine, a cheap, watery wall-coloring.

My father banked barnyard manure around the foundation each autumn. The stink faded after a while, the snow-covered manure kept drafts from under the floors and the rotted remains made excellent garden mulch in the spring. But the walls were not insulated and on winter nights when the Fahrenheit thermometer dipped to thirty below zero, the living room coal stove glowed like the hubs of hell while the bedrooms ten feet away were as frigid as Axel Heiberg Island. White polka dots of frost grew thick on the exposed nail heads. Frost jungles and palm trees twirled and swirled on the windowpanes.

For years the verandah went without a floor. But there was a real brick chimney, when many other settlers were content with a tin smokestack. And the attic was *almost* everything he dreamed of. On the January night in 1920 when he brought his bride home, he stopped her in the snowy yard. "Wait, don't go inside! Not yet! Wait here and watch!"

Then he trotted a kerosene lantern up a ladder into the attic to proudly show how light shone golden through the four dormer windows. It would never be more than a storage place and a hideout for small boys, but it gave the little house a touch of class.

And in this house one September evening I was born. It had been a crisp, amber Wednesday with goldenrod flooding the ditches and wheat standing ripe in the stook and the pasture tinged with autumn yellow. My father came in early from the fields and my mother said, "I think it's time. Better call Dr. Woodside."

He rushed to the wall telephone with its two noble, shiny bells, its receiver dangling on a long cord and its mouthpiece out-thrust like a giraffe's head. He pressed a button on the side, twirled the crank handle and roused Central at her distant switchboard. Central knew everyone on the party line, their personal quirks, their private lives, and could have ruined them all if she'd chosen.

"Central? Give me Dr. Woodside!" my father shouted. Everyone shouted on Long Distance, partly because voices did grow faint over the miles, partly because it seemed right to shout on Long Distance.

"Doctor's over at Jim Lightbody's delivering a baby," shouted Central.

Panic! My parents had already lost at birth the baby who would have been my older brother.

"Quick, Central, get me Mrs. Wilson!" my father shouted.

Yes, Mrs. Wilson, the district nurse, would come if someone fetched her. Skip Bell, one mile south, had a new Model T Ford. My father wrenched the crank, three longs, two shorts, a local call this time. And Skip, a lanky, slow-talking, Christian gentleman said, sure, he'd bring the nurse.

By nine o'clock I was half-born and my father was hysterical. He seized the nurse's hand and towed her to the house like a tug berthing the *Aquitania*. Mrs. Wilson nose-dived into the hole where the verandah floor was supposed to be. My father yanked her out and aimed her at the bedroom. Dazed but un-damaged she assisted my mother who was becoming a little distraught.

"Don't be frightened any more, my dear," soothed Mrs. Wilson. "It's over now."

Dr. Woodside arrived later to commend all participants. My birthplace was duly registered — not a village or town as for ordinary folk but "Section 10, Township 13, Range 5, West of the 3rd Meridian." I was born on the land, with the land, bonded forever to that land, that little house.

My father got busy and finished the verandah floor.

# 3

# Rock Piles and Bloody Idiots

For eighteen years that gray hunched little house was the center of my universe. I loved it deeply without ever saying so out loud. In all those years I never slept under another roof more than a half-dozen times. Only once did I travel more than twenty miles away, and then only to Moose Jaw.

It was our box seat to an endless pageant of sunrise, sunset, moonglow and changing season. You could rest your eyes forever on its view. The south bay window was always brimming with sky and the ripple of wheat fields and green brown pasture. At night pinpoints of light sprang out comfortingly from other isolated houses on other hills. On clear dew-drenched mornings the sky played tricks and the grain elevators of Gravelbourg, normally hidden from view sixteen miles away, sprang up in mirage on the horizon.

The house itself was never more than a hill's

climb from our point of vision from anywhere on the farm. When we were achingly tired or hungry or lonely we could see it waiting, our anchor and our refuge. I knew every inch of it and of the buildings and fields around it.

How, in a house so tiny, could even a boy find secret places? I did, and had slivers in my knees to prove it.

*I am travelling the hands-and-knees route this morning, keeping low to the floor because hostile Indians have been sighted in the district. I slither behind the davenport, scuttle under the round oak dining table whose droopy cloth affords excellent cover, then dash in among the geraniums in the bay window.*

*Pausing to scan the horizon for hostiles, I feast my eyes on the little panels of green, rose and beige leaded glass in the east windows, as I do a dozen times a day. They make me happy. My practical mother would have settled for plain glass, which was five dollars cheaper and easier to clean. But how lucky my impractical father insisted on colors, for on sunny mornings they cast tiny rainbows on the walls.*

*I scurry over open ground to my second hideaway under the bed, skirting beloved landmarks along the route: the two rocking chairs, the fold-up chair which sometimes folds with people in it, the wee bookcase with apple-crate shelves, the dresser my brother and I share — two orange crates with a curtain in front and doily on top — where once the cat bore her kittens in a woolly nest of socks and underwear.*

*At last: home-free in the cool, dim pantry. Hostiles never dare come here for fear of being crushed under three hundred glass jars of fruit, meat and vegetables. I lean back gratefully against the canned chicken, a small, dark*

*boy with patched overalls, thick eyebrows like my father
and a square muffin of a face.*

*"Bloody idiot," I say in friendly greeting to the dried
reddish smear on the pantry wall. The smear and I have
been friends for years and, of course, it must be one of the
bloody idiots my father is always talking about. I peek
out past my mother's skirts at the trap door, and feel the
familiar delicious prickle of terror.*

*The trap door, centered in the kitchen floor, opens on
an earth cellar full of potatoes, carrots, apples, spiders
and blackness. I know for a fact that the Devil loiters
there on his days off, waiting for a shot at me. Once I fell
in but stumbled out crablike, blubbering, with a lump on
my head but with my precious soul intact. Probably the
Devil was working in Gravelbourg that day.*

Two hundred yards from the house a creaking
windmill drew water pure and icy from 150 feet
down. When the wind failed we pumped water by
hand and lugged it home in pails. It was hard water,
laden with minerals that left a scaly sediment in
buckets and tin cups, and defied soap. My mother
added lye to make it lather on washday, but the lye
made her hands bleed.

"You're damned if you do and damned if you
don't," my father would say.

"Jack!" she would cry. "Don't swear in front of
the boys!" He would wink at us behind her back in
mock repentance.

On those years when the Lord saw fit to part with
His rain, soft water flowed directly from Heaven
down the roof to a rain barrel beside the big flat stone
that was our back doorstep. A commune of mosquito
larvae and other dancing, diving, squiggling creatures
lived happily in the rain barrel, but it was only wash

water; we casually skimmed them out and heated the water in a reservoir built into the kitchen range.

Saturday bath night was a ritual, as predictable as grasshopper plagues or the reelection of Mackenzie King. We bathed in turn beside the wood-burning range in a galvanized metal tub, big enough for a child to scrunch down in or an exposed teenager to skulk in, with one nervous eye on the undraped windows. It never occurred to us to bathe on other nights. Soft water was scarce and anyway, what kind of fanatic would bathe twice a week?

Then, scrubbed and pyjama'd, we snuggled around the fat little Galt heater with its trail of black stovepipes meandering to the living room ceiling. It had a nickel-plated footrest where we toasted our slippered soles, sang songs and told stories. On winter mornings my brother and I fled from our Arctic bedroom to dress in front of it, keeping our bare bottoms at a respectful distance after the first awful bum-sizzling burn.

The outdoor privy, a brisk hundred-yard dash to the northwest, left an indelible mark on the soul and buttocks, when hoarfrost gathered thick and picturesque around the seat. But in summer, with the door slightly ajar, we sat front-and-center on the best view in the West.

Even before my brother Larry was born, I never lacked company. Year around, huge families of English sparrows nested in our eaves, greeting each dawn in rasping monotone and crapping in methodical rows on anything and anyone below. I admired their guts — after all, it was their prairie too — but few others shared my sentiment. The sparrows held choir meetings directly outside the best bedroom, the one assigned to Uncle George Collins on his occasional trips from Moose Jaw. Uncle George, a bit of a *bon vivant*, was not used to waking at five in the morning with birdsong drilling into his hangover. It was from him that I learned the really good swear-words.

My friends included a dog or two, and sinewy country cats named Greynose or Tabby, gliding like shadows along their beat — house to trees to barn to haystack — checking for milk, scraps, mice and trouble. There were always round-eyed, cud-chewing cows, one named Reddy and another named White-face.

There were horses with distinct personalities. Old Jack was dean-of-men, a horse of infinite goodwill, who never flattened his ears in anger and always pulled his share of a load even when younger horses shirked. All he asked was kind words, oat sheaves, Sundays off and the occasional fresh, juicy corncob which, before munching, he rolled in his mouth like a Havana cigar. Tommy, the perennial teenager, was all muscle and feet with a roguish eye and a black velvet nose. Pat, the dappled gray, lean and peevish, would bite or kick me out of spite unless he wanted a favor. May — white, stubby, plodding, uncomplaining — reminded me of certain neighborhood housewives.

My associates included several hundred Barred Plymouth Rocks with red combs, shiny button eyes and rock-bottom IQs. They lurked stupidly under the horses' feet, looking for fresh manure with grain in it. Horses were always stepping on them. Then the chicken mob, like human and animal mobs since time began, tried to peck the cripples to death. My brother and I rescued and nursed them to health in a private compound known as the Chicken Hospital.

One invalid became a pet. He loved us to the bottom of his chicken heart and followed us everywhere, galumphing along on his gimpy leg, muttering affection from deep in his throat. It sounded like "Kuck" so we called him that. Having a pet chicken was weird enough; a pet chicken with a name that could be turned into an obscenity was social suicide.

One day my friend Roy Bien came by. He was four years older, a handsome, precocious, good-natured extrovert — everything that I was not. He played the guitar and yodelled like Wilf Carter. He knew the latest dirty jokes. He could dance. Girls liked him. He was allowed to work in the fields, a symbol of manhood. I would have crawled over hot coals — no, I would have *gone down in the cellar* — to win his approval.

Now he said, "That's a funny-looking chicken."

"That's Kuck," said my brother, too young to understand the value of lying.

"That's WHAT?" whooped Roy Bien, sensing a bit of madness that would convulse our school friends for weeks to come. In one-tenth of a second I had to choose between losing Roy Bien's favor or selling out in front of my brother.

"Uh . . . we call it . . . uh . . . *Cluck,*" I mumbled apologetically. "Because it makes that . . . uh . . . funny clucking noise. Y'know?"

"Oh yeah, Cluck," said Roy Bien, immediately bored. My brother looked strangely at Kuck and me, wondering which was the chicken, but kept his silence and let me save face.

Some days, happy in my solitude, I roamed among the farmyard poplars, maples and stubby caraganas or along pasture trails worn to dust by generations of horses and cows. *This is Saskatchewan. Sask-at-chew-an.* I loved the feel of it, the wild Indian cadence on my tongue.

Some of our land was just as those Indians had left it. In a sheltered grassy hollow I found circles of stones that had anchored Assiniboine and Plains Cree tepees a half century before. Sometimes I crouched in the circles, giddy with the thought that those Indians and my family were maybe the only humans ever to have trod this place.

An outcropping of quartz thrust itself from a certain hill; I christened it my diamond mine. Beside the Long Slough — where spring runoff lingered long after other waterholes had run dry — clung a stunted scrub willow. I scrunched under it and pressed my cheek to its gnarled trunk. It was the only wild tree on our farm — a survivor like us.

There were rock piles wearily picked and stacked by my father and inhabited by generations of gophers, skunks, rabbits and mice. I had soft, crumbly, yellow rocks for writing tools and smooth, black rocks for slates. There were rocks so great that they defied all the pickaxes, crowbars, chains and straining teams of horses, and so they stayed, flinty obdurate islands in the wheat fields. Sometimes when the grain stood high I hunkered down on a jutting rock pretending it was a hut with a paved floor and bamboo walls. And always when the fantasies were over, my real house was waiting.

Far from cities and the main railway line, I knew little of hobo camps, breadlines, riding the rods or Depression riots. The unemployed were mere faces, taut beaten faces in Regina *Leader Post* news photos, not people I knew. Barely into my teens when the worst years were over, I never truly understood the tense murmurs through those paper-thin walls after bedtime, as my parents fretted over the money we never had.

We had enough to eat, although it was plain, and enough to wear, although it was plainer. I had no yardsticks for poverty and so no envy. We had our land and we had the house, our fortress against the world. I thought we were the luckiest people on earth.

# 4
## Cavalier

Farming was an ordeal for my father. Some days he could not even work a pump handle without losing his breath. The veterans' medical board had assured him that the spot on his lungs was nearly cured.

"How are you feeling generally?" they asked.

"Fine," he lied. A Brian O'Lynn never admits weakness to bureaucrats. So, with pension board logic, they cut his stipend from forty to twenty-five dollars a month.

Although the pension dwindled even more, he refused to touch his forelock to doctors or government lackeys. (Years later he also refused to apply for the old-age pension — he was then seventy-two but *thought* he was sixty-seven — until he learned that Prime Minister Louis St. Laurent was taking it.)

With the same flinty stubbornness he tilted with the farm, and was knocked down again and again.

Often he came in from the fields black with dust, and fell on the couch too exhausted to wash, although he was a fastidious man. Horses crushed him against barn doors. Jouncing ploughs threw him in stony fields. He broke an ankle, had a thumbnail torn off, had a hand slashed by a mower blade, and cracked his ribs more times than we could count. But he never gave up.

For a few years, when the nearest grain elevators were forty miles away, he and his neighbors made the thirty-two-hour round trip with horse-drawn wagons full of wheat through cold autumn drizzle, never knowing if the price would be worth it. Once, in Moose Jaw, he stood all night holding a land-office doorknob, as a lineup grew behind him. When he went to the toilet another man seized the door, but he wrested it back and got a piece of the free land offered to veterans.

He was far better suited for some bookish job. He loved to write in a bold, black script, all scrolls and flourishes, rather like abstract art, and equally hard to understand. The community called on him for chores that required a modicum of learning. When the neighboring village of Shamrock sponsored a weekly movie he ordered the films, kept meticulous accounts and manned the box office, all without receiving or expecting pay. During the thirties he doled out relief codfish, coal and clothes to the needy. For years he served as secretary-treasurer of the rural school board, where his ethics kept him constantly in hot water.

He believed in integrity, the Royal Family and the Conservative party, in that order, and stood ever ready to defend a lady's name. It was no accident that he joined the cavalry during the war, or that his favorite book was Alexandre Dumas' *The Three Musketeers.* He was a cavalier in high-bib-overalls.

He quarrelled bitterly with one neighbor who accused a teacher's unwed cousin of living in sin. Even when the girl became demonstrably pregnant my father did not unbend. Another teacher broke down when a farmer threatened to sit in her classes to see if she were fit to teach his offspring. My father told him, in less than friendly terms, to go back to his chickens and pigs, and lost another friend.

Over a quarter century he managed to feud with most of our neighborhood men and several wives. Some refused ever to speak to him again. During elections, when our home was a polling station and my father a deputy returning officer, most warring neighbors swallowed their pride and passed through our portals with surly grunts. But one arranged to be registered at a polling station miles out of his way to avoid the hated house of Collins.

In all these imbroglios my mother was an uneasy bystander. "Jack, those teachers are going to move away sooner or later," she pointed out. "We have to. *live* here." But he never slacked his principles nor understood why others bore long grudges. He invariably turned sunny as soon as he'd made his point.

He was equally single-minded about debt. He hated it. He worried about paying taxes when no one else could or did. Once he became physically ill at the thought of begging a fifty-dollar bank loan to buy binder twine. He repaid the government for all the relief coal and livestock feed given him during the Depression. When he posted the farm for sale in the 1940s his advertisement announced "Clear Title." It meant Collins had paid off his mortgage. No one but my mother truly understood how proud he was of that.

One night at Shamrock's movie she won three dollars as a door prize. She was ecstatic; she could run her house for a fortnight on three dollars. My father drove home in a black cloud. What if he, as movie organizer, were suspected of rigging the draw? A week later, reluctantly, she publicly donated the money to the skating club. Only then did he smile again.

His pride sometimes puzzled and annoyed me. In the mid-thirties I had a Regina pen pal, Ian McLeod, who after one exchange of letters surmised that I was below the poverty level. He sent a half-dozen postage stamps to further our correspondence and promised me a box of his mother's oatmeal cookies. My father was incensed — "WE CAN TAKE CARE OF OURSELVES!" — and made me return the stamps. McLeod was miffed, terminated the friendship and, worst of all, cancelled the cookie shipment. I refused to speak to my father for two days.

But he and my mother through trial and error learned to live in perfect tandem. He would gladly bankrupt himself to buy treats for the people he loved. She clutched her pennies with a grip of steel. At a time when their sole cash income was his pension — then down to fifteen dollars a month — he gave her ten dollars for housekeeping. She never spent it all, always holding back a dollar or two for "emergencies" or to buy him a Christmas or birthday present.

Her quiet strength buoyed him up on black days. When his spirits were high he swept us all with him on a tidal wave of good cheer. He was always the first man up on a dance floor, a five-foot-nine Fred Astaire until his breath gave out. Songs burst forth from him: "Tipperary," "My Wild Irish Rose," "Mother Machree," "Brian O'Lynn" of course, "Lillerbuloo" (an old Irish ballad), and sometimes this wry cocky World War I ditty, perhaps from the London music halls:

It's all right
It's all right now
Nothing is the matter any more
They said
The Army wasn't strong
Everything went wrong
Until the day I came along
And then the bands played
They all hoo-rayed
The Kaiser, they say, turned deathly white
Cause I joined the Army yesterday
So the Army of today's all right.

Even then I realized my parents were not perfect. Her will was too ironclad for less dedicated humans. His temper and biases ruffled many feelings including, sometimes, mine.

Yet from them my brother and I learned so much: how to cope, how never to give up, how to salvage fun from the simplest things. Without her we might not have survived; without him we might have missed the enchantment of life.

They loved and supported and complemented one another. They were "spoken for" through all their years together and, together, nothing could defeat them. Anything other than being together was unthinkable.

Only once did I ever hear them in a serious quarrel, over what I never knew. He was sick and hurting and raging at the world that day, and she stood in the kitchen with sobs that stabbed my heart.

It ended quickly — but it was the first of only two times in all those years that I ever saw my mother cry.

# 5

## "Yuh Don't Owe Me Nuthin' "

One Saturday night in the Gravelbourg movie house Hugh "Tim" Adams imprinted his manners forever in my consciousness. As we strolled past the GENTS washroom en route to our seats, Mister Adams (as we boys were taught to call him) turned to my father, Larry and me and murmured gently, "Shall we make ourselves comfortable?" It took me a moment to catch his meaning; then I was agape with respect. Such *style*.

Butch Gwin would have said, "Ya wanta take a leak before the show?" But it was not fair to compare Butch and Tim, except that both were my special friends.

Mister Adams, Shamrock village postmaster, had a soft, cultured English accent, a crisply trimmed Neville Chamberlain moustache and a brown, nubbly tweed suit with matching cap. Wilbur "Butch" Gwin, whose one-room shack crouched like a gray bug on a hill a quarter mile east of us, wore a three-day stubble on his cheeks, and his belly rose hard and round as a keg of nails beneath the bib of his GWG overalls.

No two men were less alike; yet, next to my parents, they were the favorite adults of my childhood. They could be counted on always, instantly, without question.

Mister Adams and his wife, Eva, were English gentlefolk: she, immensely practical and ever smiling; he, gracious and literate. As a musician, book lover and owner of a shortwave radio, he was my cultural mentor. He coached me on the violin for a village talent show and played the piano accompaniment while I hacked and sawed my way through the thickets of "Londonderry Air" to first prize (appropriately enough: a medal left over from a track-and-field meet). Afterward, with his eardrums still reverberating, this civil man rose and thanked *me*.

It was he and capable Eva who dropped their work to speed over the dirt roads one afternoon and tape up my father's hand when a mower blade cut it to the bone. It was Mister Adams who brought us music books from the city. He shared my father's reverence for the Royal Family. He was Shamrock's symbol of taste and breeding.

Butch had little education and few social graces — shortcomings that he tried to mask with a pseudo-gruff manner. But among people he trusted, people who did not patronize him, he was full of humor. His laugh, born somewhere around his size 13 work boots, came shaking and heaving through his thick frame, escaped in a mighty wheeze like a runaway balloon and ended with a booming "HAR HAR HAR!" that brought tears to his eyes.

His voice — normally a gravelly rattle — soared over the hilltops when he was chastising some errant

horse or cow: "HIYAR-OUTTATHERE-GODDAM-
SONABITCH!" Butch had no telephone, my father
was no mean shouter himself, so sometimes they
braced their heels and exchanged brief messages over
the quarter mile.

Everything about Butch was big, from his gener-
ous nose to the pores in his skin. Six feet tall and 220
pounds, he could hold up a wagon single-handed
while other men slipped a wheel off its hub; hoist the
entire side of a granary off the ground using a post for
a lever; tuck a hundred-pound sack of Robin Hood
flour under each arm without working up a sweat.
When my father was ill Butch never failed to help.
Afterward my parents always said, "What do we owe
you, Butch?" And always, unless it was specified
work-for-hire, Butch growled, eyes rolling with
embarrassment, "Aw, yuh don't owe me nuthin'."

All the same we evened the score. Butch had carte
blanche at our dinner table. It was only one of several
on his regular beat, but once a week or oftener he
arrived unbidden at mealtime. My mother always
said, "Butch, will you stay to eat?" And Butch,
playing the polite charade to the hilt, always replied,
"Well . . . don't mind if I do, Miz Collins." Larry and
I were always delighted to see him. We envied his
muscle, his appetite (he always ate seconds) and his
Bennett Cart. The Bennett Buggy — named after the
prime minister who had the rotten misfortune to help
usher Canada into the first years of the Depression —
was a horse-drawn automobile sans engine and
steering wheel, a rolling bit of rural ingenuity. Butch
cut it down to a two-wheel cart and drove at full
gallop, standing up, a southern Saskatchewan Ben
Hur.

Sometimes he took us for rides, or showed us how
to make whistles out of grass blades, or let us lick the

glued edge of his Chantecler cigarette paper after he'd hand-twisted a Bull Durham cigarette. He never ignored or talked down to small boys; there was much boy still in him. When his barn was infested with mice Larry and I ambled over with Greynose IV and Tabby VII. For two hours man, boys and cats squealed and capered together, and a mouse ran up Butch's pant leg. One July 4 our Uncle Dorlan came from California, laden with exotic gifts, including the first firecrackers I'd seen. Their bangs echoed among the hilltops. For a full hour Butch stayed away, his manners fighting his curiosity, until manners knuckled under.

"Figgered there was some Yankees over here," he wheezed triumphantly. Naturally, we shared our supper and fireworks with him.

He might have enjoyed a family of his own, but that was idle speculation. Butch invariably struck out with girls, and it was easy to understand why. One day he lolled, rolling a smoke, in our second-best wicker rocking chair (the solid oak rocker was my father's, by law). "Horseback ride!" cried Larry, age five, and hopped aboard Butch's crossed leg. Then, face puckered, he sprang down.

"Phew, I smell *feet!*" he shrilled. My mother blushed. My father said tartly, "So sit somewhere else." Butch chuckled indulgently. What was a little body odor among friends? No male among us used deodorant. Butch had never had a woman's nose to live up to. And, as he grew less and less fastidious, he never *would* have a wife or housekeeper (the latter, in some cases, being synonymous with "wife").

Yet bachelorhood did not seem to ruffle his good humor. It may even have enhanced it. No sharp soprano voice ever ordered him to pick up his dirty socks, straighten his posture, reduce his waistline, go

to church on Sundays or trade in his Bennett Cart on
a Model A Ford. The community's finest cooks
catered to his palate. Small children looked up to
him, and he enjoyed their company without having to
keep them in cod liver oil, school books or Sisman's
Scampers. Butch was free — and maybe the smartest
man among us.

# 6

# A Homely Shabby Lot

Although Butch and Tim were my favorites, I enjoyed most of our neighbors. Even the sourest would help a friend in need. (In our case there was always a qualifier to that little truism: they'd help *if* the neighbor in question were speaking to my father that day. Our family gained and lost diplomatic recognition more often than a small Balkan state.)

When my father returned from the war, his neighbors took up a collection to buy him a gold watch. On second thought, they reasoned, fifty acres of ploughed sod was more practical for an invalid, and sensibly spent the money on that. None of us ever locked a door. A neighbor might want to come in for a phone call in our absence; many could not afford their own phones. When shipments of relief coal arrived in Shamrock, my mother climbed a hilltop at a prearranged hour, faced west toward the home of Andrew Costley (no telephone) and wigwagged a dishcloth over her head. A mile away on another hill Costley's housekeeper, Sarah Greer, waved acknowledgment and soon Costley's wagon joined others jogging into town.

There was never enough money for school teachers' salaries, so the neighbors paid off in food: one gave home-baked bread; another, fresh eggs; a third, fresh butter; a fourth, potatoes and carrots. Locked together as we were by the Depression, neighborliness was a matter of survival.

Yet always we clung to a quaint formality. Women rarely called other women or men by first names. After twenty-five years my mother was still "Mrs. Collins" to her good friends "Mrs. Bell," "Mrs. Smart," "Mrs. Curtis" and "Mrs. Hagstrom," and to all their husbands. Perhaps this solemn propriety helped their friendships to endure.

We were a homely shabby lot, nothing like the coiffed and carefully tousled actors on today's television versions of the thirties. Our hands and faces were burnished brick-red by sun and wind, with hat-lines, neck-lines and squint-wrinkles etched in white. Men let their whiskers grow two or three days and their hair two or three months.

When we finally broke down and had haircuts they were clipped skin-tight, to last another two months, leaving a fresh white band of untanned flesh. Since barbers charged as much as forty cents, a wife or child often wielded the clippers and shears, with maybe a saucepan over the subject's head to get the sides even. Most of us looked like Larry of the Three Stooges, the one with the bowl-shaped head.

It was not a time of blatant sex appeal. One or two malicious virgins of my acquaintance wore sheer stockings rolled just above the knee — allowing, on windy days, a maddening glimpse of bare flesh. But the average female calf was swathed in sexless cotton shades of Taupe and Caribou. Loose homemade dresses rose high to the neck; I was eighteen before I *heard* of cleavage, much less saw it.

If the women were drear, we males were a sight to drive them to a nunnery. In winter — encased in Penman's fleecelined or Stanfield's all-wool long johns, with dropseat and a regiment of buttons down the front — we shuffled lumpishly, itchily, across our Dr. Zhivago landscape in buckled overshoes or shin-high felt boots, wiping our noses on the backs of our mittens. Day in, day out, we toiled in flannel shirts buttoned to the neck, steel-shod boots stained in horse manure, and patched GWG overalls. (Our denims, by the way, were never patched or faded *on purpose*. New, rasping, blue overalls were a mark of affluence; every man and boy coveted them.)

From the waist down we resembled refugees from a Russian soccer team: our pants bagged voluminously from hip to ankle. Whoopee Pants were a passing fad (they had colored wedges inserted at the cuff for a bell-bottom effect), too impractical for the farm. Bell-bottoms quickly lost their flair when weighted with cowshit.

We boys were dressed on the three-year plan. For the first season everything was too big. "You'll grow into it," mother always said. She was right: the second year everything fitted. Last came the year of exposed wrists and ankles.

Winter or summer, only a madman or an Easterner went out bareheaded. Depending on sex or season, we were crowned in cloth cap, babushka, straw hat, railwayman's striped cap or the bowl-shaped fur or blanket-cloth cap later known in the armed forces as the Piss Pot. For a couple of seasons World War I aviators' helmets were in vogue for boys. With our little round leather-clad heads protruding from bulky sheepskin coats, we looked rather like newel posts. We were drab, but alike in our drabness, which was comforting.

We spoke not with an accent but a distinctive tongue. True, Andrew Hagstrom's Swedish upbringing turned my father's first name into "Yack." Tom Hawkins (Irish), Walter Smart (Scottish), Arthur Curtis (English), Bill Bien (German-Russian) and Albert Fortin (French) all contributed to the multilingual stew. (Albert, being a friend and neighbor, was never classified as a "Pea Soup," which was what we called the people of Gravelbourg, our French-Canadian town to the south.)

But nationality was irrelevant. Pronunciation and turn of phrase were the keys to our togetherness. A scholarly outsider was instantly known by his failure to mangle the language. To be one of us, it was imperative to know that a coyote was not a "*ki*-oat" or "ki-*oaty*" but "*ki*-yewt"; that a goalkeeper was a "goolie," a creek was a "crik" and "youze" was the plural of you.

"Goin' like sixty" or "Really goin' to town" implied enormous speed and energy, as did "Like a dose o' salts through a tall Swede" and the ever-popular "Like shit through a goose." "She'll do" meant that a car, a fence or a situation had been repaired to an acceptable level. To "fix his wagon" or "fix his clock" was to even a score with him, once and for all. Bad weather, the universal conversation-starter, was best described with "It's really comin' down out there" or "She's rainin' (snowin', blowin') like Billy-be-damned." A good crop was a "bumper." A female spouse was "The Missus" or "The Wife." A boy's father was "The Ole Man."

We stayed on our farms for private and assorted reasons: we couldn't afford to move to The Coast or the Peace River Country (mystic places so distant and revered that they were pronounced in capital letters); or we were too stubborn; or we simply loved the elbowroom of Saskatchewan. Space allows a man to indulge his idiosyncracies, and each of our neighbors contributed a fragment — a small kindness, a foible observed — to the sum total of a boy's growing up.

Farmer John Eib to the south of us, for instance: why did he never unclench from his yellowing teeth the evil-smelling curved pipe that never stayed alight? Did he not know it was eroding a notch in his molars? Probably he did but, I realized long after, it was his security blanket. And why, in moments of rage, when other men found relief in "Lord-sufferin'-jumped-up-jeezes-snarlin'-snappin'-arseholes," did Mr. Eib merely shout, "By Harrys!"? After, I guessed it was from the old English oath, "By the Lord Harry." But at the time I thought he was saluting Harry Lauder whose *burrrrring* Scottish songs Mr. Eib let me play on his hand-cranked gramophone, before he served homemade ice cream on the long, drowsy, sun-baked, fly-buzzing, Sunday-go-visiting afternoons.

And why did wee dour Andy Costley eat the eggshell along with the egg? I never knew, because his Scottish accent, filtered through a troublesome upper plate, was incoherent. But I guessed — knowing that chickens and other birds swallow grit to help grind their food — that Andy was storing sharp stuff in *his* gullet to give the store-bought teeth a hand.

What brought chubby, cheery George Marriott from England to his windswept farm, when his lively mind and bent for natural science might have graced some university? Lucky for me, whatever it was. He told me the origins of strange rocks and let me pore over his collection of Indian arrowheads laid bare by dust storms. One stifling summer night over iced lemonade (we never had ice but resourceful Marriott had a straw-insulated icehouse stocked from the creek in winter), he produced the first binoculars I'd ever seen and said, "Have a look at the moon, Bobby." I'd been looking at that flat silver Halloween face in the sky for ten years; what else was there to see? Suddenly my eyes were full of a new, rumpled, shimmering landscape. I couldn't speak for the glory of it but Mr. Marriott saw it shining from my eyes.

Why were the women of our neighborhood so patient, so resourceful? Partly because they had been trained to believe in hard work, the brotherhood of man and the superiority of the particular man in their lives. Some of those men were, I suppose, brutish chauvinists. One took umbrage at his wife's cooking and flung her stewed beans on the floor. She, instead of wrapping the empty dish around his head, patiently cleaned up the mess. But the rest of us were scandalized: most women were equal partners, whether wives or housekeepers, and generally seemed happier and more resilient than their men.

Miss Greer, for instance, did a normal sixteen hours' work per day in Costley's home and garden, kept him stocked in eggshells, played a thunderous "Road to the Isles" on her accordion, danced the Highland Fling when coaxed, and kept tins brimming with oatmeal cookies and brown-sugar candy for small visitors.

All of us revered saintly white-haired Auntie May Walker, who was incapable of uttering a harsh word. Straight-backed and frail, old yet ageless, British accent precise, faded dresses somehow elegant, she might have stepped from a nineteenth-century wa-

tercolor. Her long face, her very spectacles, twinkled
with goodwill. But Auntie May had an underlay of
steel, which kept her spirit intact and shored up her
bachelor brother Donald, whose house she managed.

Donald, as prickly and trouble-prone a man as
I've known, was all craggy cheekbones, obstinate jaw
and bushy eyebrows. Like my father, he could be
sunny one minute, outraged the next. Inevitably, they
quarrelled over school board trivia and refused to
speak for years. Sometimes they met, driving in
opposite directions on a lonely road, and passed with
averted eyes.

Before the feud the Walkers and my parents
exchanged Christmas Day visits, always ending with
interminable whist games. My father and Auntie
May were pitted against Donald and my mother. Mr.
Walker hated to lose, rarely did and gloated over
every win. Auntie May's game never improved.

"Oh dear me, partner!" she would chirp apologetically. "I seem to have trumped your king again!" My
father could never prove it but was sure kindly
Auntie May was throwing the Christmas whist games
to keep Donald's terrible temper in check.

If so she was wiser than we knew, for Donald
needed all the victories he could get. Like my father,
he should never have farmed. He had a flair for
misfortune, as when a friend found him on the roof,
cleaning his chimney from its west side while facing a
stiff east wind. Glaring down, furious eyes blazing
from blackened face, Donald roared, "WE'RE IN A
HELLUVA FIX!"

Packs of mischievous small boys plagued him,
because he rewarded their pranks with rage. At
Halloween they tipped over his privy, or moved it off
center, hoping Mr. Walker would fall in the foul pit

in the dark. Once they perched his buggy on his barn roof.

Horses also conspired against him. There was a style and mystique to handling a team. A good wagon driver held the reins nonchalantly, preferably in one hand (to impress wives, sweethearts or even enemies) but with a firm authoritative touch, standing in a semislouch with feet well braced, addressing the horses with a cluck of the tongue. Donald drove slack-reined and all elbows, standing ramrod straight, his Piss Pot rising from his head like the dome of a botanical garden, ear flaps at right angles.

"GEE! HAW!" he bellowed, urging them right or left, unconvincingly. The horses sensed he was not in control. They humored him, when it pleased them; then — the roll of an eye, a flash of equine ESP and — runaway! One afternoon they pitched him out and my school friend, Billy Bell, a shy, sturdy boy, became an instant hero by vaulting into the wagon box and muscling the runaways to a halt. Mr. Walker somehow survived all of those wild headlong gallops, ending up with only a few broken bones or bitter cries of "BLOODY HELL! BLOODY HELL!" as he faded into the distance.

Sometimes a soupçon of drama brightened our days. Nephew Jimmy Walker arrived for a visit, fresh from the British navy. At a schoolhouse dance he twirled the pretty teacher around the floor more often than her local boyfriend deemed proper. The boyfriend picked a fight — a grave tactical error, considering the knockabout reputation of sailors.

"I had to lay him out," Jimmy Walker explained ruefully to his aunt the next day. Much later Auntie May, the pacifist, realized that her nephew had not merely lifted and gently lowered the fellow to the floor.

"He had to *strike* him!" she told my mother with awe.

Violence was rare; when it brushed our quiet community we were thunderstruck. A mile north of our house, young Teddy Smart lived in a tiny unpainted shack on a half-section farm. He was bright, polite but a loner; he and I exchanged no more than a dozen words in a dozen years. In winter he moved in long, loping strides across the fields, a gray-clad ghost against the snow, tending his trapline and visiting his parents two miles distant.

One night as he lit his coal-oil lamp a .22 bullet ripped through the window into his chest. His high-bib-overalls saved his life: the bullet ricochetted off a metal button, leaving only a flesh wound. Quick as a flash Teddy blew out the lamp. Outside, a horse galloped away. Teddy calmly staunched the blood, hiked to his parents' house and phoned the police.

In the morning, while our party-line phones jumped off the walls, the Mounties easily tracked the culprit through the snow. He was no accomplished assassin, just a young man desperate for the money Teddy earned from weasel pelts (which rumor said was hidden in his unused wall telephone). The boy went to prison and Teddy went quietly on with his life — still wearing high-bib-overalls.

For days our neighborhood was aghast. A shooting! Even robberies were unheard of. One autumn my father hired a silent pinch-faced stranger from northern Saskatchewan to drive our binder and stook wheat. After he went away we discovered he'd pried a dollar and change out of my tin savings box. A dollar was a lot but what hurt most was that a man who had shared our home and table had robbed a piggy bank while we were at church.

We and our neighbors clucked and exclaimed over that tiny incident for a week. It was more than illegal. It was — well — just not *neighborly*.

# 7

# This Cruel and Lovely Land

Early one April afternoon in 1931 the sky turned sullen black. Our housewives knew the dust storm drill: slam doors and windows, light coal-oil lamps, cover the butter. This was a bad one. By two o'clock our teacher began phoning parents: "Will you fetch your children? I'm afraid they'll get lost going home."

My father plodded glumly through his own and Skip Bell's land — most of it was up in the air — to escort me home. My mother, agonizing for the crops and us, peered fretfully out the west window. At last we loomed through the curtain of dust. I was frisking ahead, happily plucking the first purple crocuses from the Sahara of our pasture. I was a child of the Depression. Dust storms — well — didn't everybody have them? The first flowers of spring were what mattered.

That was my Saskatchewan — cruel and sensual

by turns. Our living room walls were hung with cutout pictures from calendars and magazines: woodland streams, English stone bridges, billowing oaks — the kind of landscape we wished we had. Outside, naked telephone poles marched single file beside tedious dirt roads, and gray fence posts leaned crazily into the double-strand barbed wire, like drunks tottering home in the arms of friends. Yet deep down — I know it now — I loved our prairie best. It was uncompromising. It was magnificent.

The wind and sky orchestrated our moods. The wind played the tunes, the sky lit the stage. Together they could make us laugh or cry. When the sun shone, our spirits turned to green and gold. I lay in the yard on my back, staring deep into the sky until it whirled, and spun me with it.

The clouds came, legion upon legion, darkening the pasture sloughs and casting shadows on our souls. We looked to the sky for portents. Did that black cloud carry rain or dust or hail? Would that change of moon from Full to Last Quarter, as noted on the Wheat Pool calendar, bring a change of weather? My father thought it would, and the moon proved him right often enough.

And the wind? It never rested. It strummed the telephone wires; I pressed my face hard against the poles, rubbed silvery gray by the years, and listened to their song. The wind ebbed and flowed through the whispering poplars, churned up blizzards, flung clouds pell-mell to Manitoba. Its rough hand riffled the heads of wheat and foxtail. It lashed the stagnant water in Long Slough, booted prickly balls of Russian thistle end over end, and lifted the tail feathers of matronly hens who clucked with embarrassment. Some people were driven to suicide by the wind. Some of us were soothed by it, and still are.

I knew so intimately the smells and tastes, the language and rhythms of the land, that even now, if I were dropped there not knowing time or date, I could say, "This is a February afternoon because the long shadows always slant off the sharp snowdrifts, just so, at four o'clock" or "This is August because August always smells of sage grass and ripening wheat."

The seasons ran their cycles, as sure as life and death. Spring was best, with its sudden, softer kiss of wind, its first crows hacking and coughing in the treetops. Then a rush of warblers, flickers, swallows, blackbirds, ducks and grebes, once a robin, a bluebird, even a Baltimore oriole, all with their madrigals of hope.

The meadowlarks hunched on fence posts, drab and round-shouldered until they sprang into the sky with a flash of brown ascot and golden breast. Redwing blackbirds bickered in creaky-hinge voices. Great broad-winged hawks came sledding down the wind, their shadows panicking our squawking hens. Gophers rose up from winter hibernation with their cheerful dumb-guy expressions, and welcomed the sunshine into their hides.

The earth was fragrant with new, green life. I dug my grubby fingers into soil built up, grain by grain, from ancient seabeds and by restless glaciers a zillion sunsets ago. It came up in my fist, a damp, crumbly ball, our hope for another year.

If we were lucky, rain came after the seed was in, turning the gumbo roads to pudding and filling sloughs to their brims, until the farmers' tobacco-stained smiles cracked through their three-day whiskers. Yes! Maybe *this* would be the year, by God, the year of the bumper crop!

There were no death-dealing chemicals then to make us weed-free and sterile. The ditches over-flowed with black-eyed Susans, milkweed, ragweed, pigweed, stinkweed, wild roses, wild sweet pea and purple Scotch thistle. We picked wild bouquets, gathered pigweed to cook like spinach, and chewed tiny, red rose berries — rose hips, we called them — laden with vitamin C.

July. Now the slough bottoms were baked dry and cracked in squares like chocolate brownies. On the southern horizon Skip Bell's house danced in heat waves. Freckles broke out on children's noses. Barn swallows pirouetted in the air around little mud nests glued to the eaves. The horses on their Sundays off stood languidly in pairs, nose to rump, obligingly swishing bulldog flies from each other's nostrils. Cicadas dinned in our ears. The pasture lost its emerald sheen and the wheat withered or ripened depending on whether spring rains had come. Good Year or Bad? By now we were getting an inkling.

September. Goldenrod billowed from the ditches. It was my flower, no one else's, because it always bloomed on my birthday with the dull shimmer of hammered brass. Small, undernourished pumpkins glowed orange in the fading garden. Fat potatoes cloaked in clay came up on our spades and tumbled into burlap bags. In the cornfield stripped of its ears, the cows roamed fat and greedy, stuffing their jowls with cornstalks, munching, drooling and blessing us with moist, adoring eyes.

Even the winters had a bitter kind of beauty. Sometimes two rainbow sun dogs escorted the sun, refracted through a frigid haze. Coal smoke plumed elegantly from every chimney on every hilltop. In the white-clad stubble fields our shaggy horses burrowed into strawstacks overnight and looked out in the morning with white whiskers and false eyelashes of hoarfrost.

The frost painted palm trees on our windows and the wind sculpted snowdrifts into tiny Alps. Larry and I scooped out snow caves and huddled in them. How could the Eskimos build snow-block houses? Ours always collapsed. How did the Eskimos survive a winter? A half hour in our cave and our joints froze up.

At night the telephone wires, thickened with white rime, moaned like lost souls and the fields glittered with diamonds under the crystal moon. We skated under that moon, its cold light bouncing off the white hills, silhouetting our black swooping figures against the silver ice.

Just when we thought it would never end ("Eight months o' winter, four months o' hard sleddin'," the old-timers said *ad nauseam*), icicles sprouted from the eaves. Larry and I plucked them and sucked the ends until our mouths turned blue. Or we squared off, ice rapiers in hand, and played D'Artagnan and the Three Musketeers. Every hollow twinkled with blue water. Gossipy ducks V'd in from the south. The first meadowlark poured out his liquid song and the prairie said, "Now, let us begin again."

The prairie was a wild creature. We lived with it but never really tamed it. Turn your back, grow careless for a moment, and it would lash out. When snow rubbed out familiar landmarks a walker could easily be lost on a black night. In most places you met a barbed-wire fence, sooner or later. But one bitter night Miss Greer came bewildered to our door. She'd made a wrong turn in the dark and crawled through several wrong fences toward the light that was not her own. Another neighbor woman, not so lucky, wandered helplessly into open prairie beyond fences, and died.

One afternoon when I was four I called cheerfully from my favorite bay window perch, "Look at the pretty fire!" Instantly, my parents were running. My father had burned a strawstack and *thought* he'd seen the last embers die. Now wind was fanning flames through a stubble field toward open grass. If it reached the grass it would run wild. Prairie fires were still the terror of the country.

The horses were loose in the pasture; no time to catch them and plough a fire guard. My parents seized pails, burlap bags and me, and ran for the stubble. They planted me on burned ground ("Stand on the black and *stay* there!") and frantically pounded the flames with bags soaked in slough water. They stopped the fire just short of the grass, and walked home slowly, trembling.

Later, with grass ploughed under, prairie fires were no more. But we worked and reworked the land, taking crops out, never putting nutrients back in, leaving no trash cover to foil the wind, and the prairie got even.

The first bad dust storm raced into our district in May 1930. My father slammed the barn door, slipped the windmill out of gear so the gale wouldn't drive it to pieces, and ran for the house with dust devils at his heels. For an hour we huddled by lamplight, my parents' faces white and set. After, we went out to view the ruins of our world. There were great, ugly, empty patches in the newly sprouted crops.

The storms became routine. Some men stubbornly worked on in dust so thick they could barely see the horses' heads. Dust seeped under ill-fitting doors and windows. Auntie May Walker packed her window sills with wet towels. Some mornings we woke to find our linoleum-floor pattern hidden in dust. On the worst days we ate meals from a covered table, diving under a tea towel for a slice of bread or dab of butter. At school we cleaned the floor with a shovel.

Any grain that survived such storms was too stunted to be properly tied into sheaves. But Russian thistle always flourished. The tough prickly weed ripened and broke away from its roots; the wind rolled it onto the fence; the fence vanished under tons of thistle and sand. Phlegmatically, we learned to put thistle to work: dried, as bedding on stable floors; green, as cattle fodder. It gave them explosive diarrhea which they shared with anyone foolish enough to stand close behind them.

The animals' plight was the real tragedy of the Depression. Half of my father's pension went for horse and cattle fodder. Sometimes we had to feed them a subsistence diet of plain straw soaked in molasses and water. As their body resistance fell low, they were infested with lice. We doctored them for that and all their other ills. There was no veterinarian; we couldn't have afforded one anyway.

Life with those animals was always tinged with pain. When a horse kicked and killed our favorite dog, we four solemnly buried him under a tree, and my father removed his cap as for a human friend. The calves that we petted and pampered grew up to be slaughtered for beef. When horses grew too old or sick to work we could not afford the luxury of keeping them — except, for a while, the beloved Old Jack. Forty years later, remembering it, my mother was still close to tears. "We had to shoot them," she said. "It seemed the kindest thing to do. . . ." Butch did it for us; it was one of the ugly realities of farming that neither my father nor any of us could face.

# 8

# My Enemy,
# My Friend

It was late March, usually, when his squeaky-door whistle came shrilling down the wind. I spotted his flat, furry head in the early morning sun, rising upright from his burrow, eyes beaming curiosity, his back as straight as a sergeant major's, streaky brown coat a bit tacky from a winter underground, his country-yokel front teeth hanging out.

My friend, my enemy, the gopher — back for another year.

I ran shouting home to report the news, and to enter "First Gopher" beside "First Crocus" in my little *Signs of Spring* notebook. My parents responded with thin smiles. They knew — *I* knew — that hundreds of his kind would soon be playing hell with crops and garden. And I, like every other red-blooded prairie lad, would be out with club and snare, dog and gun, trying to kill him for the government bounty. And yet — it was so good to see him. He was life; he was spring; he was Saskatchewan.

We were ambivalent and often inconsistent in our attitudes to the ecology. Larry and I nursed an injured meadowlark until it could fly again. Once my father carefully cultivated a safety island around a killdeer's nest in an open field, while the nervous mother ran with a dragging wing, trying to lure him away. Often we found horned larks' nests in the pasture, guarded them from cats and dogs while the eggs hatched, then dropped grasshoppers into the yawning pink mouths until the scrawny babies fell back sated.

Yet a red-legged hawk cruising the clouds sent us running for the .22. Hawks were known chicken killers (although they rarely got one). Fortunately for the hawks, we were terrible shots.

We hated the grasshoppers that blackened the summer sun and stripped the crops, year after year. We loathed the army worms that marched in a mindless gray green carpet across fields, roads, railway tracks and up the sides of houses. We plunked potato beetles unceremoniously into deadly buckets of kerosene, and snipped in half with scissors the fat, green caterpillars that ate our maples.

It was open war with trap and gun on coyotes and weasels because they too ate chickens. But they and the hawks would also have cleaned up the rodents if we'd given them a chance. Instead we tinkered with nature's balance and so we had gophers: big, little, old, young, whole dynasties of gophers, cute as a Disney cartoon, flirting their saucy tails and merrily eating us out of house and home.

Nothing, with the possible exceptions of grain elevators and the word "Saskatchewan" itself, so caught the Easterners' fancy and inspired so many bad jokes, although few really knew what a gopher *was*. In fact he was *not* a gopher but a Richardson ground squirrel — *Spermophilus richardsonii*, to give him his Latin name. But every boy knee-high to W. O. Mitchell knew a gopher was a gopher and if the name was wrong, too bad. Blame it on the explorers. Then, as now, the gopher lived in a "honeycomb" (*gaufre*, in French) of tunnels and — well, it could have happened so easily. . . .

Scene: The explorers, Pierre de la Verendrye and his sons are trudging across the plains in search of the Western Sea. Pierre stumbles, falls and clutches his ankle in pain.

Son: "*Qu'est-ce que c'est, mon vieux?* W'at 'appened, dear old dad?"

Pierre: "Damn *gaufre* 'ole!"

Whether or not it really happened that way, zillions of gophers were frolicking around Carlton House, near what is now Saskatoon, when Sir John Richardson noticed them in 1820. Having found nothing else that day, Sir John announced the discovery of the Richardson ground squirrel. By the turn of the century pioneer naturalist Ernest Thompson Seton had learned far more about *Spermophilus richardsonii* than anyone wanted to know.

The gopher was twelve inches long with a three-inch tail, Seton revealed, habitually dug one front door and up to seven back doors, and used his flat head for pushing dirt through the tunnels, but not for much else. "Dull witted creature," wrote Seton scornfully; he also branded the gopher a coward, after putting one in a cage with a Franklin ground squirrel and a striped ground squirrel. While the other two shadowboxed and squeaked insults, the gopher sat glumly with his head in a corner, wondering what Seton was trying to prove.

For, in truth, the gopher was and is a family man, a home-loving pacifist. He rarely strays more than two hundred yards from his hole, likes to sleep in (from October to March), and raises nine-to-eleven children every year. Once Seton dug into a gopher labyrinth and found a cosy sitting room lined with grass and oat hulls. One can picture the gopher resting there, with his feet up, after a hard day in the fields.

But *Spermophilus richardsonii* is undeniably hard *on* the fields. The diligent Seton once searched the cheek pockets of a dead gopher (it had been waylaid, en route home from shopping, by a hawk) and counted 240 grains of wheat plus nearly 1,000 grains of buckwheat. Over the years other researchers added to the gopher's crime sheet: he has fleas, which can transmit bubonic plague; he has ticks, which transmit Rocky Mountain spotted fever and tularemia; and he and his kin can eat $3 million worth of grain in a year.

So, governments began issuing free gopher poison to farmers and, in my day, offered a bounty of one to three cents per gopher tail. The great prairie gopher hunt was on. Men, women and children trapped gophers, snared them, drowned them out with water, pinged them with .22s and poisoned them with strychnine mixed in oats.

Motorists in Model Ts wildly pursued fleeing gophers in deep road ruts. Some piped automobile exhaust down gopher holes. One man set small explosives in the burrows, crying savagely as geysers of earth showered around him, "*That* oughta get the little bastards!"

The gopher's insatiable curiosity worked against him. Any clever boy could whistle the beast out of his hole and into a binder-twine snare. My friend Kerry

Wood, an Alberta naturalist, once told of seeing two coyotes sucker a gopher with the well-known Coyote Squeeze Play. One chased the quarry down a hole and made a noisy show of growling and digging. True to form, the gopher couldn't resist sneaking up a back door for a look. The second coyote nailed him.

I had mixed feelings about the carnage. The first time I tried the water-and-club technique, inexpertly attacking the poor half-drowned creature that emerged, I was overwhelmed with shame and grief.

"It was *bleeding!*" I told my father brokenly that night, and he understood. But then we discovered that Jiggs, the terrier, would kill gophers swiftly and relatively humanely, once routed from their holes. So my brother and I collected gopher tails like everyone else. It was our only pin money. Anyway, a boy who didn't hunt was scorned and despised by his peers.

Perhaps we had to vent our frustration on something in the Depression years and, Mackenzie King being out of reach, the gopher was convenient. One afternoon our school inspector, Mr. Loeppky, came to see my father. This large, calm, literate man was clearly a notch above other mortals because he wore a suit and tie on weekdays. I quaked when his heavy bald head and steel-rimmed spectacles swivelled on me; he seemed to be reading my mind, and finding it wanting.

But that day he found me catching gophers in the pasture. In a twinkling Mr. Loeppky stripped off his coat and vest and joined in with such sweaty zeal ("Now we've got him, now we've GOT him!") that I realized he was no god, just a gopher addict like the rest of us.

The ghosts of gophers past may be comforted to know that we never much diminished their numbers. They went on through the decades raising nine-to-eleven children every year; eating wheat, oats, barley, rye, clover, wild onions, gardens and, for protein, the occasional cricket; and setting their biological clocks for March to rise bright and cheery for another year.

Agriculturalists in Saskatchewan now tell me that they expect never to eradicate the gopher, just to keep his numbers down. He is the consummate prairie survivor. And sometimes still, in the lengthening light of a March morning, I cock an ear, half listening for the gopher's call. How else can I be sure it is spring?

# 9

# Helpin' the Ole Man

Never in all those years was there a real holiday
— a week at a seaside or a cottage or *anywhere*. Never
did we escape the treadmill of work for more than a
day at a time. It was work or die. Nobody could
survive for long in those days on government hand-
outs.

Incredibly — now even I find this hard to believe
— I *yearned* to work like a man. "He's a regular little
man," my father would say proudly, when I was very
small. Obviously, manhood was admirable stuff. My
schoolmates confirmed my hunch. To stay home and
work like a Little Man was every boy's dream.

*"How come you wasn't here yesterday?"*
*"Yah, well . . ." (a nonchalant glance into the middle
distance and — hock-ptuiii — a Little-Man-size dollop of
spit into the schoolyard dust) ". . . I was helpin' the Ole Man
with the summer fallow."*

I fought like a panther for the right to help the Ole Man (although I never dreamed of calling him that). I pleaded for the back-breaking labor that, forty years later, Canadian farmers begged young men to do for board, room *and* $180 a week — and were refused. I wanted to be a muscular illiterate, respected by my peers. To my disgust, my parents usually insisted on schooling.

There was another satisfaction to our labors, less easy to explain. The risk in farming was maddening, and yet . . . exhilarating. Take a pail of fresh, foaming milk and, hey-presto! Suddenly it was butter, cream and drinks for boys, calves, chickens and cats. That black field of fresh, damp furrows, dappled with Franklin gulls scavenging for worms: with a little rain, luck and a prayer or two, it turned into Thatcher wheat, bowing golden in the wind. That barren garden, monochrome gray, surely dead forever: pamper it with countless hand-lugged pails of water and interminable hours of hoeing and fertilizing, and suddenly one morning — green shoots cracking through the crust. Always, that little miracle of growth-again filled me with foolish joy.

And so, year in, year out, the gambler in each of us went back for another shake of the dice over the land. We had no tractors, power combines, milking machines, refrigerators, freezers, microwave ovens, automatic washers — no electrical appliances of any kind. Everything was driven, nagged and coaxed by man-woman-boy-and-horse power.

*We tread two endless wheels of labor on this farm, one within the other: a daily round of chores spinning inside the greater circle of seasons' tasks.*

*It is morning in the barn. In summer, early sunbeams laden with motes of dust slant through the knotholes. In winter, a smoky coal-oil lantern throws its amber glow amid the flickering shadows. A choir of sparrows is chanting the "Anvil Chorus," off-key as usual.*

*As always, we milk Old Reddy and Whiteface by hand. It is an art. Beginners pinch the cow's teats instead of squeezing them, and are admonished with a whack on the head from a shit-caked tail. But long ago we learned to milk by reflex action, capped heads propped against the warm flanks, minds dreamily fixed on other chores ahead, the ammonia stench of manure stabbing our sinuses.*

*Milk dings and hisses into the pail in rhythmic double time; you can tell a good milker by the cadence. Old Reddy placidly munches her cud, pleased with the deft performance at her nether regions. Greynose VIII, Tabby XI and Jiggs the dog hover near with limpid eyes, begging a taste. I aim a stream straight into their mouths. I pour a serving for the silken little calf. He sucks greedily on my milk-dipped finger that simulates his mother's teat, until he learns to guzzle directly from his bucket, impatiently butting his white, furry hammerhead against the rim.*

*The kitchen is a medley of breakfast smells: eggs frying, bacon crisping, thick homemade bread toasting directly over the cook-stove coals, steaming oatmeal the color of cement but delicious with brown sugar and cream — a breakfast to quell a man's snarling stomach until at least mid-morning.*

*But first my brother dumps milk into the Vega cream separator and cranks the handle to a high-pitched whine. Out come a trickle of cream and a separate torrent of milk. Morning, noon and night we drink fresh unpasteurized milk and pour thick yellow cream on peaches, pie, mashed potatoes, bread pudding — you name it, we cream it.*

*"I could eat shingle nails if you put cream on 'em," my father announces at least once a week. Perhaps our veins are clogged with cholesterol. Who cares? We've never heard of it and we're blissful in our ignorance.*

*Breakfast over, Mother pours cream into a tall, earthenware churn with a long-handled plunger. Thump-thump-thump — a half hour of woman-or-boy-power and suddenly yellow clots of butter are sloshing in buttermilk. She scoops them out with a scrubbed wooden paddle and pats and squeezes them into a one-pound mold. The buttermilk is a treat for Butch Gwin or the chickens, whichever gets there first.*

Chickens ruled our lives. In the middle of each spring night my mother pulled a coat over her nightgown, stumbled groggily outdoors by the light of a pale, astonished moon, made her way down the path to the tune of a million crickets and the lonely, distant yodel of a coyote, and checked on the health and well-being of three hundred newborn chicks in their oil-heated brooder house. They were far more trouble than human babies. Each morning three hundred pairs of shoe-button eyes rolled up reproachfully from downy, black heads and three hundred pink throats uttered piercing tin-whistle cries.

"What is the meaning of life?" they shrilled. "Why did we leave our warm embracing shells? Where is the woman with the corn-wheat-oats-and-barley mixture, the chopped hard-boiled egg with oatmeal, and the sour milk? We are no common chickens, we are purebred Barred Plymouth Rocks!"

All summer they had to be fed and watered twice daily and guarded from hawks, coyotes, weasels, disease and their own innate stupidity. The meaning of life, if they wanted to know, was very basic: eggs from purebred chickens sold for up to eighty cents a dozen when shipped to a Moose Jaw hatchery, while ordinary eggs brought only ten to fifteen cents at the village store. It therefore behooved these future hens to lay furiously upon their coming of age, lest they find themselves appearing as the main course for Sunday dinner.

*Monday morning is wash day. It has been wash day back through generations of mothers, grandmothers and great-great-grandmothers with red and wrinkled hands. To wash on Tuesday, say, or Friday would violate God's ultimate plan for the universe.*

*Our washing machine is a wooden vat atop a clutter of cogs and gears. My mother fills it with tubsful of scalding water and stirs in curly shavings of Fels Naptha Soap, whittled from a yellow bar harder than a taxman's heart (but at three bars for twenty-five cents, a bargain too good to resist). Then, if school is out, I push-pull an upright wooden handle, which twirls some gears, which turn the agitator, which makes the washer groan "heeere weee gooo," as loath to begin as me. Slowly its creaking parts warm up and so do mine. At last the whirring gears shout "HEREWEGO HEREWEGO HEREWEGO" as my arms fly with the handle and I bury my mind in the nonsense song.*

*On sunny summer days the clothes dry outdoors and come in smelling of clover-on-the-wind. On sunny winter days they freeze solid (here's a perfect frozen suit of Penman's underwear, arms and legs outstretched, waiting for a perfect frozen man). On stormy days they hang indoors on a maze of cord. Larry and I plunge screaming up and down the steamy aisles until our mother's famous patience snaps.*

*"YOU BOYS! STOP IT!"*

*We subside, sniggering evilly over oatmeal cookies and milk, as she tests the flatirons heating on the stove. She moistens a fingertip, flicks it on an iron — sssss — the iron's ready. How does she do that every time and never burn her finger off?*

*She harnesses our mischief with more work. We trim lamp wicks so they'll burn with even wedge-shaped flames, and we polish the fragile lamp globes with crumpled newspaper. Sometimes we help our father clean stovepipes and come in black with soot, flashing white smiles like the pictures of Amos 'n' Andy in the* Saturday Evening Post.

One year we forgot to clean the stovepipes. Early one autumn morning my father staggered out on the front porch in his pyjamas and fainted. I followed him, vomiting. Mother and Larry, sleeping closer to windows, rose up only slightly less ill. The stovepipes were clogged; a smouldering coal fire had filled the house with noxious fumes. That afternoon I walked alone far out in the fields in a late October chill, took a picture of our house with Mother's bulky box-Kodak, and shivered at how close we'd come to never seeing that view again.

*It is early spring. Every man and boy west of the Third Meridian is afoot with pitchfork and matches. Everywhere the sky is smudged with puffs of smoke. Some strange satanic rite? No, we're raking and burning the masses of Russian thistle that clung like scabs to the fields all winter — the first official labor of spring.*

*Next we shuffle seed grain through a hand-cranked fanning mill to sift out weed seeds. Then: seed the fields, cultivate the remaining land to lie fallow and rejuvenate itself over the summer, mow the grassy slough bottoms, and pile the hay around the barn in conical stacks.*

*It is lonely, private work. Hour after hour, uphill, downhill, shifting numb buttocks on hard metal seat, watching sweat stains grow under the horses' collar pads. Hot sun scorching your back. Dust seeping down your neck, into your eyes, into your pores. Horses breaking wind in your face. Acrid stink of sweaty armpits. Clank of steel against rock. Swish of pitchfork. Hay fragrant as peppermint.*

*Lots of time to think. Of what? For a boy: of girls,*

*learning to drive a car, hitting home runs. For a father: of whether it will rain, whether there'll be money enough to move to The Coast, whether your kids will ever get to university, whether the goddam Liberals will get in again, whether you'll make it through this bloody day to wash off the dirt, eat a good supper, sing a song with the kids, talk it over with The Wife before tumbling bone-tired into bed.*

Our way of work was pitifully slow and inefficient but there was a pleasure in horses that no machine could match. We talked to them constantly; they answered with a tolerant twitch of ear or knowing sidelong glance. We fondled them and scolded them and they gave back love or pique. In early morning as they stamped in their stalls we curried away their dried sweat and itches, and combed out tangled manes and tails until their eyes glazed with ecstasy. Then we garbed them in harness, a ritual as precise as the crowning of a king: oval leather horse-collar; maze of straps, buckles and chains all with names and functions — martingale, hames, bellyband, traces; last, the hateful bridle, its steel bit so foreign to their mouths. We warmed it by the stove or in our hands on winter days so it wouldn't cling to and tear their tongues, but rare was the horse that didn't resist with clenched teeth like a child refusing rice pudding.

Once — nicely harnessed but not yet hitched to the wagon — Pat and Tommy, the terrible twosome, ran away on me just for the hell of it. Hitched together, off they pelted at a full-gallop, one on either side of a barbed-wire fence, for a half mile. When I led them home, unharmed, all three of us were trembling: they, because they knew they had sinned; I, because they could have been cut to ribbons.

On rainy days the horses had a holiday but we

kept working. Broken harness to patch. Stones to pick — the earth shrugged new ones to the surface as fast as we hauled them away. Fences to mend: digging post holes through flinty soil with a hand-auger, tamping in posts with a crowbar, stretching the barbed wire taut with chain-and-pulley, hammering staples, going home with torn hands. A thousand maple, poplar and caragana to be cultivated (each of these trees originally hand-planted by my parents).

Lavish though we were with time and energy, we were painfully frugal with materials. My father straightened and reused each bent nail. For a missing bolt he substituted a twist of haywire. If coal and wood ran low we burned cow chips (dried manure). After butchering the winter's beef we made lap robes for the sleigh from cattle hides. The fat was rendered into laundry soap.

Each scrap of string and brown paper from Eaton's parcels was saved and recycled. The catalogue itself and the *Leader Post* were our only toilet tissue. Kitchen slops nourished the flower beds. Vegetable peelings went to the chickens; they returned the favor with manure for the garden.

Once a cloudburst flooded the chicken coop. We hustled fifty soggy, inert bodies into the house. Half of them revived around the kitchen stove. Mother quickly transformed the rest into canned chicken and their downiest feathers into pillows and quilts. A coyote raided the coop one night, killing a dozen out of sheer bloodlust before he fled from our rifle. They too were hastily plucked, cleaned and cooked. Waste was sin.

My mother was a virtuoso at "making do." She performed endless sleights of hand with bleached Robin Hood flour sacks. Crouched over her ancient sewing machine, foot pounding the treadle that made it run, she turned sacks into shirts, dresses, dish towels, tablecloths, doilies, pillowcases and opaque windows for chicken coops. The hens couldn't have cared less about a clear view of scenic Saskatchewan, as long as they could see well enough to fill their bottomless stomachs.

She found wild cucumber vines growing along a distant creek, brought home seedpods and soon had a leafy perennial arbor clambering up our verandah. She used Squirrel Peanut Butter pails for lunch buckets, Empress jam tins for flowerpots and leftover baked beans for succulent sandwiches. In summer she mixed gallons of a cheap, thirst-quenching drink from vinegar, sugar and water. In winter she made ice cream from custard and whipped cream, quick-frozen on the back step.

She and the kitchen stove were always in cahoots. Together they produced great, brown, crusty loaves topped with slicks of melted butter. Brown-sugar cookies. Cakes of infinite variety, long before cake mixes were known. Eggs in every conceivable guise. Pies of rhubarb, apple, raisin, pumpkin, custard and lemon. Every autumn, with the stove raging hot and damp hair plastered to her flushed face, she canned three hundred quarts of chicken, beef, corn, peas, beets, rhubarb and whatever imported fruit the budget allowed.

Her ragbag was a symbol of our times. There was always a ragbag under the bay window: a bleached flour sack (naturally) stuffed with clean ragged socks, shirts, dresses and underwear — an Oriental bazaar of tattered silks, satins, denim, polka dots, stripes, floral reds and royal purples, all tumbled together awaiting further duty. They served interim roles as costumes for plays or ribbons for cats, until reassigned as patches for elbows and knees, or as hooked and braided rugs.

And as we sat by the kitchen table in the evenings, watching to see what she'd contrive next, I began to understand that even work was a kind of ragbag: sometimes turning out as mundane as an elbow-patch, sometimes as creative as a rug with a red-rag rose growing from its center, but always as good or bad as you chose to make it.

# 10

## The Holy Harvest

Some people dream of violent death. For Floy
Leona Hartzell Collins the ultimate nightmare — she
actually dreamed it — was to run out of food at
mealtime. It happened only once, in the first pen-
urious year of their marriage, but it branded her for
life. Ever after, she cooked gargantuan feasts that
brought even Butch Gwin to his knees.

Once every year her prowess was pushed to its
limits. It was that heady time when the land paid off
(or was supposed to), the season scented with rich
cookery, cigarette smoke on autumn breeze, sweat,
dust, the first nip of frost, wheat, axle grease, tractor
fuel and hope, all rolled together into the grandfather
of all smells: Harvest Time!

It was the one time I was allowed to stay home
from school. Through spring seeding I sat in a school
full of girls, the last eunuch left in the harem.
Through summer fallowing I was still there, the Cree

warrior disgraced and barred from the hunt. But bless you, Lord, for sending me the holy harvest. I was out there in the thick of it, a bona fide Little Man.

Oh, the drama, the worry, the importance of it all! The moment grain ripened it had to be harvested before rain, hail or early snow rotted or flattened or buried it. Our ancient Massey Harris binder refused to be hurried. It had suffered too many humiliating plunges into hidden badger holes, too many rocks cracking its cutter-knives, too much green Russian thistle clogging its gears. It was a tired, mean ornery-old-man of a binder. Almost daily it balked and stuttered to a stop. The horses waited, hitched to it, heads down, half smiles on their lips, thanking that Great Horse on high for this lucky unscheduled rest, while my cursing father or a bemused hired man patched the binder's broken innards with haywire.

Then, for a while, it slashed merrily through the standing wheat, spitting a stream of snugly tied sheaves almost as perfect as those in Saskatchewan's official coat of arms. Man, woman or boy followed on foot, building stooks; wheat-sheaf tepees to keep the grain dry; eight to a stook, butts rammed firmly into the stubble, heads locked smoothly together to shed the rain; each row so arrow-straight that twenty stooks looked like one. (Thirty years later in an Ontario friend's field I proved with childish delight that I was still an impeccable although short-winded stooker.)

At last, the grand finale of our working year — threshing.The threshing crews travelled from farm to farm. They were composed of young neighbors graced with instant manhood and itinerant strangers from *far* away — ten miles, even twenty. Their arrival was as carefully staged as a Broadway opening.

They trotted teams and bundle wagons single file

up our driveway, controlling the reins with one hand, caps slouched indolently over eyes, spitting methodically whether or not they had anything to spit. From the front steps my brother and I watched with humble eyes, silently begging a nod of recognition from these harvest knights. They studiously ignored us, except Butch Gwin who beamed a lopsided whiskery grin.

Behind them, belching splendid, foul fumes of grease, oil and exhaust, a thundering Case tractor towed a potbellied International Harvester threshing machine. At the wheel stood Butch's solemn older brother, Elmer. He stood as a matter of style during this grand entrance, although the Case people had thoughtfully provided him with a seat.

Elmer was withdrawn, almost melancholy, among humans. Words crept from him reluctantly, as though each departing phrase shortened his life. But he could make a motor sing. Soon his threshing machine was parked in the field, mumbling savagely to itself like some demented dragon, joined flywheel to flywheel with the tractor by an umbilical cord of leathern belt.

His teamsters peeled off among the stooks, building unbelievable loads as high as they could reach, and shameful it was if a man's load collapsed. Back beside the monster they fed sheaves into its chomping jaws; it slashed the twine and spewed a golden plume of straw into a mounting strawstack. Screens and shakers husked the wheat and moved a gushing, burnt-orange stream into the waiting granary. There it was: our payoff for the year. My father hovered anxiously, chewing and fondling the kernels, testing their firmness and weight. Good Year or Bad? He looked to Elmer for clues, and found none.

Sad-eyed and silent, Elmer ministered to cogs and gears with his oil can.

The threshers worked from dawn to last wisp of dusk, whetting appetites that drove housewives into nervous fits. Would there be enough to eat? Would the men like it? The threshers shamelessly rated each woman not by her looks but by her skill with a skillet: this one roasted beef that melted on your lips like a lover's kiss; that one baked pie crust like Portland cement; a third — ah, this was the cruellest cut of all — "couldn't cook bait for a bear!" They were the kind of men who would eat and tell. They could make or break a woman's reputation.

No woman among us was more prone to pre-threshing jitters than my mother. As a bride she had erred in her first harvest: on the bad advice of an equally green English housewife, she'd served *stew* for *breakfast*. The men had eaten it sullenly. ("Stew! What the Christ she tryin' do to us?" "Aw, give 'er a chance, she's a Yank, y'know.")

After that she swore never to fail the threshers' taste buds again. Each year from the moment they arrived until the last bundle rack jogged out of sight, she moved at a half trot, catering to their growling stomachs.

She and my father were up at four in the morning. By six they had set out a breakfast of champions: porridge, bacon and eggs, stacks of bread, mounds of butter, two or three tins of jam, fried potatoes, fruit and cookies. The men clomped in from their mobile bunkhouse, redolent with fresh green hay (which served as mattresses) and ancient body odor. They dashed water on their faces from a tin basin, combed their hair with their fingers and huddled on planks set around the elongated dining room table. Platters of food appeared, dwindled, vanished. Voices rumbled and bantered, but, by tacit agreement, there was no swearing and no dirty jokes in a woman's home. As they filed out on a wave of nicotine a few big shy boys, not long away from their own mothers, mumbled, "Thanks, Miz Collins," eyes fixed steadfastly on their feet.

All morning my brother and I slaved like coolies, performing with smiles the chores we loathed in other seasons: hauling water, peeling potatoes, shelling peas, husking corn. We were *harvesters.* It freed our mother to wash dishes and cook another major meal by noon. This was dinner: roast beef or chicken, innumerable bowls of carrots, peas, corn, mashed potatoes and gravy, tea, coffee, always two kinds of pie — a quarter pie per man and seconds if they wished — plus cookies and cake to fill the empty spaces.

She whipped up the same spread for the evening meal but with a different meat: if beef at noon, chicken at night. At three in the afternoon Larry and I helped carry sandwiches, coffee, cookies and cake to the field, lest the threshers fall writhing from starvation before supper.

My parents never got to bed before eleven and my mother never stopped fretting. One morning, in the hurricane's eye of the Depression, down to her last gram of ingenuity and out of normal pie filling, she made carrot pie. The stewed and strained carrots, topped with whipped cream, looked and tasted rather like pumpkin. But they were not pumpkin and a couple of gourmands in bib-overalls *did not finish their portions.*

When they left the house my mother was in shock. Would the crew bad-mouth her through the Rural Municipality of Shamrock and on into the Fourth Meridian? Would our family ever survive the shame? Could she face the men at supper? Should she flee to the United States?

Then Tony Gwin came back, rapping on the screen door. He was yet another brother of Butch, even taller and rounder. His normal conversational tone was a shout. But his perpetual scowl masked a friendly disposition and Tony was not without guile.

"SOME OF THEM WAS SAYIN' THEY DIN'T LIKE YER CARROT PIE, MIZZUS COLLINS," Tony shouted.

My mother winced.

". . . BUT I SEZ TO THEM, I SEZ 'THAT'S THE BEST CARROT PIE I EVER ET, ANYBODY DON'T LIKE THAT PIE OUGHTA BE KICKED OUTA THE HOUSE!' "

"Really, Tony!" beamed my mother. "Would . . . would you . . . like another piece?"

"DON'T MIND IF I DO, MIZZUS COLLINS."

She sat him down at her kitchen table, cut him a half pie smothered in whipped cream and poured two cups of coffee. While she watched, entranced, Tony wolfed it down and smacked his lips.

"THANKS, MIZZUS COLLINS," he roared, and returned to the fields. His menacing stare put an end to snide remarks about her cuisine. And she went singing at her work all afternoon. Suddenly it wasn't drudgery any more.

# 11

## Going to Town

Those dewy-morning mirages that lifted Gravelbourg, ghostlike, onto the southern hilltops, could not have picked a worthier subject. A French-Canadian Brigadoon on my horizon.

Gravelbourg the metropolis (well, a nine-elevator town was no ordinary, ratty whistle-stop). Gravelbourg the historic, founded by the pioneer priest, Gravel. Gravelbourg of the thousand wonders: a cathedral, live Catholics, "Pea Soup" spoken on the streets, and a hospital run by gentle, wrinkled nuns who fed me some ice cream after relieving me of my tonsils.

So many riches Gravelbourg had. Mounties (regrettably, dressed in everyday brown, and riding cars; but you had to settle for second best in the Depression). An actual lawyer named Ted Culliton who knew my father by name and was that most rare and treasured of species, a Liberal my father liked. A barbershop where one man and two sons could get haircuts for ninety cents total. A movie house where $1.50 admitted the entire family to see *Rose Marie.* Was there ever a Mountie with eyes so blue and jaw so granite as Nelson Eddy? Was there ever an Indian Love Call like Jeanette MacDonald's? For Butch the movie's ultimate moment came when Rose Marie, stranded and famished in the bush, had to swallow her pride and, with it, beans. (". . . And she said she din't *like* beans. . . . HAR HAR HAR. . . .") Somehow, the eating of hated beans brought the ethereal Ms. MacDonald crashing down to Butch's plane.

Better than all of these pleasures, and the happy ending of any day in Gravelbourg, was a meal at the Paris Cafe. Every four-elevator town or larger had a Chinese restaurant named Paris Cafe, Elite Cafe or Gem Cafe, but always called The Chink's. It was run by thrifty hardworking men who served filling meals laced with indigestion. Their premises were steeped in eternal odors of black-fried eggs and scorched steaks. In their kitchens, surely, they feasted on delectable egg rolls, won ton soup and Moo Guy Pan, but to us that was heathen fare. We demanded Occidental food and we got what we deserved.

No matter. For me the sheer wonder of dining out made up for the assault on my alimentary canal. As we crossed the Paris Cafe's holy threshold a babble of Chinese and an odor of burnt fat issued from the kitchen. We slid behind marble-top tables with wire-back chairs — ice-cream parlor furniture of the sort young matrons now eagerly cart home from antique shops. The heavy white crockery always included a tiny butter dish, just big enough to hold a single pat. The table knives had heavy white handles. The drinking glasses were thick enough to survive the occasional Saturday night brawl.

I always ordered Brookfield sausage, the Rolls Royce of sausages, filled with genuine pork instead of bread crumbs. Roast beef, chicken — I could get that ordinary stuff at home. My Brookfield sausage with mashed or fried poatoes, canned peas, soup, all the butter and doughy bread a boy could eat, raisin pie (on which the West was built) and a beverage came to forty cents. Expensive, but we only did it once or twice a summer.

Why did we so rarely visit this citadel of delight? Because Gravelbourg was sixteen and a half miles away — a full day's round trip by horse and buggy — *and* it was an RCMP post. The latter point was significant. Even if we could coax the 1929 Chevrolet to run, we couldn't afford license plates. The Mounties turned a blind eye on this transgression only if we stayed out of their bailiwick, or sneaked in when they were out of town.

So usually we settled for Shamrock, five and a half miles north. If the roads were dry my father drove the green Chev gingerly, distrustfully, never once goin'-like-sixty, and leaned on the horn, "OH-OOO-GAH," at all obstacles within five hundred feet. Such caution was not like him, but he hated machines.

The village had two main streets, arranged in a T. Atop the T lay Shamrock's *raison d'être:* the Canadian Pacific Railway tracks. Some towns were built on rivers; Shamrock's river was two ribbons of steel. Both our nameless main streets had boardwalk down one side, a measure of their importance. Nameless lanes and alleys scrambled behind them.

For a three-elevator town Shamrock had few of life's necessities: no doctor, dentist, barber, bank, hospital, library or beer store. For years there was a one-room jail but no cops or criminals. It finally became a summer home for the United church minister, an event I swiftly turned into a news item for the Moose Jaw *Times Herald* for two dollars. There was a lumberyard, blacksmith shop, community hall, municipal office, post office and a couple of farm machinery agencies — all weatherworn frame structures with the weary apprehensive look of a TV-western town just before the gunfighter rides in.

The train crept snaillike down the branch line: on Monday from Moose Jaw to Swift Current, on Tuesday back again, on Thursday and Friday more of the same. It hauled out wheat and hauled in letters, days-old *Leader Posts*, relief hay and coal, overalls from Eaton's, apples for the general store, machinery parts, lumber, everything we could not grow or make ourselves. Most of us fitted our trip around train time, making it a social outing too.

The sixty-mile rail trip from Moose Jaw to Shamrock theoretically took four hours but the train was always late. We cursed its tardiness every time, but secretly relished the chance to loiter. The CPR agent tilted back his green eyeshade, listened to the chattering telegraph and reported, "She's gonna be an hour late. Just pulling outa Coderre now."

So we sauntered down the dirt road to visit Bill Lynn, elevator agent. While I inhaled the dusty tang of wheat and craned my neck at the elevator's mysterious heights, Bill Lynn and my father exchanged views (happily identical) on how the Liberals were driving the country to hell in a handcart.

Then on to Charlie Peterson's blacksmith shop to get a ploughshare sharpened. There in the dim and smoky murk — black iron, blackened walls, only the red eye of a forge gleaming angrily through the gloom

— the squat and soot-stained smithy was in harmony with his environment.

Sometimes, at whist drives or concerts, taciturn Charlie appeared uneasily with his Sunday suit; he never seemed to be *in* it; they were uncomfortable fellow travellers. Black hair hung shaggy on his forehead; grit lurked in his pores and fingernails no matter how hard he scrubbed.

But in the shop, in his grimy workclothes with a leather apron shielding him from sparks, his forearms thick as other men's shanks, Charlie shed his awkwardness. Now this stubby silent man was all poetry of motion: fan the flames alive with bellows; heat the ploughshare to cherry red; pluck it out with tongs and onto the anvil; *pound-clang, pound-clang,* sparks blossoming as a sharp, new cutting edge grew under the sledgehammer. Then an angry dragon's *hissss* as he dunked it in a tank of water and laid it steaming on the floor.

"There she is, Jack, watch 'er, she's still hot."

At last the train came. First a mushroom of smoke far behind the hills. Then the whistle, no puny diesel "peep" but a full-bellied "AHHHHHWOOO-WOOOO" riding the wind. Then a thrumming of rails as the little train chuffed into sight, self-importantly, pounding the steel at thirty miles an hour, pretending it had held this blinding speed all the way from Moose Jaw instead of lingering around Courval and Coderre and Trewdale like one of the unemployed.

A tide of farmers, dogs and refugees from the pool hall surged to the platform. The train thundered in, billowing smoke, bell clanging insanely, brakes screaming, and ground to a jolting stop. Faces peered out from the single coach — world travellers bound for who knew where? Sometimes a local homecomer climbed down, strangely alien in city clothes.

The trainman, playing to a full house on the platform, became a model of CPR speed and service, flinging out mail bags and freight at a headlong pace. The local drayman supported this charade, heaving bags onto his wagon like a man possessed, then needlessly galloping his team three hundred yards to the post office. The train moseyed west toward Kelstern, and was quickly forgotten as the fickle crowd sprinted for mail. Elbow to elbow in a narrow corridor we watched our glass-fronted mailboxes while, in behind, Hugh and Eva Adams stuffed the slots with letters, catalogues, magazines. Until, at last, a world of far-off relatives, wars, politics and glossy magazine people with clothes that fitted and all the Brookfield sausage they could eat, tumbled into our hands through Box #43.

We turned back down the boardwalk, fast-stepping with averted eyes past the pool hall (a known place of sin and decadence where my parents would not let me set foot until I was sixteen) to the final stop: Slim's General Store.

If it had not been for his free calendar each year I would never have known his real name. It was discreetly printed between the date pad and the mandatory picture of rosy-cheeked farm girl with pet calf: "W. K. Yuen, General Store, Shamrock, Sask." Even so, none of us bothered to wonder what "W.K." stood for. He was just "Slim" or "The Chink" — one of us, yet never one of us.

Year in, year out, he awaited our pleasure behind his polished wooden counter with its glass showcase and its orange wheel of cheddar cheese. He was tall, thin and slope shouldered, with sad eyes and a lurking half smile always ready to burst into a grin.

His head announced the seasons: salt-and-pepper cloth cap in winter, cream-colored straw fedora in summer, worn indoors and out.

Slim had begun with a restaurant but was such an incredibly bad cook that he turned to storekeeping. That, too, was a wretched occupation. Every family needed groceries but few could pay regularly so they cajoled or bullied Slim to spin out their credit. He survived by living alone on the knife-edge of poverty, shaving prices and tolerantly letting customers' bills pile up until they sold a side of beef or a load of wheat or a dozen eggs and, he hoped, paid off.

I prowled his store like a grateful bloodhound, sniffing the spoor. Here, the oiled-leather aroma of new harness dangling from hooks. There, the virgin scent of new blue denim stacked high on shelves beside khaki drill work shirts and striped police braces at twenty-nine cents each. Out back: the sharp, oily tang of kerosene in a barrel; Slim filled our little can and shoved a small potato in its nozzle in lieu of a cork.

Under the counter: a madcap aroma of peppermint sticks in glass jars, chocolate maple buds, licorice allsorts, twisted red and black licorice sticks, Oh Henry bars, and cookies sandwiched around enough pink icing to rot all your molars for twenty-five cents.

High-ceilinged and cool in summer, warm as a mother's hug in winter, Slim's place was one of four village oases. Youths with raging acne, their pompadours Brylcreamed to a blinding gloss and cigarettes pasted to their lower lips, found comfort in the pool hall. Sturdy lads with bruised knuckles and dirty fingernails lined the walls in Harold Robinson's garage and worshipped motors. Shy men issuing one-syllable weather reports ("Jeez, cold out there") hung around the blacksmith shop. Families met at Slim's.

The women could spin an hour's worth of gossip out of a sixty-cent grocery list. Men surrounded the fat coal stove, winter or summer, spitting, lying, griping — whichever they did best and liked most. Kids with five-cent coins extracted five dollars worth of sucking and burping from a bottle of Orange Crush or Cream Soda. Slim seemed to enjoy the company, contributing many smiles but little conversation. Sometimes when we paid our bill he leaned across the counter to press a paper bag of jelly beans in my hand.

"Li'l boys like candy," he chuckled every time, with a twinkle of gold tooth.

How *lonely* he must have been. No one, to my knowledge, thought of inviting him home for dinner. Sometimes he appeared at community socials, standing uncertainly against a wall, his half smile cocked and ready. Sometimes on weekends, when he could afford gas for his old car, he drove at breakneck speed to Moose Jaw where he had friends.

Yet we too were his friends, in our own absent-minded way. When the government doled out relief cheques to needy families, Slim was at first not allowed to accept them because, a rumor went, he was peddling illicit booze. The government, cloaked in righteousness, frowned on that until my father and cousin Charlie Vesey drove Slim to the city and cleared his name.

And when he finally announced he was going away — to China, perhaps? I wonder if anyone asked — the village gave him a farewell party. A little crowd gathered in the community hall with cake and coffee, sandwiches and gifts. At first Slim refused to come. At last Mrs. Lynn, the elevator agent's wife, fetched

him, blushing, chuckling, drowning in embarrassment.

The gift he liked best was a signet ring with the
initial *S.* I never knew if it stood for Slim or
Shamrock. The latter, I hope, because shy, patient
Slim, so eager to be friends, was for me part of the
pleasure and indelible memory of going to town.

# 12

## The Mexie, and Other Great Inventions

*We are galloping headlong over the plains, the two of us, circling Long Slough, heading toward Wild Tree where a half-dozen rustlers are hiding out. They are hired guns, desperate men, wanted by every law enforcement officer in the West. We are heavily outnumbered but not afraid.*

*"I theenk we have to keel them, eh amigo?" The Mexie hollers cheerfully over the thunder of hooves.*

*"Si!" I pant, exhausting my Spanish vocabulary. "Draw yer gun, Mexie!"*

*It is quickly over. As always, The Mexie and I are too fast for them. . . .*

My friend Pedro Gonzales — The Mexie, to his intimates — was a boy for all seasons. Steely eyed, darkly handsome, quick to defend me in a gunfight and shrewd enough to hush his mouth when I was talking, he was instantly there when I needed him and instantly gone when I didn't. All of this was easy for Pedro Gonzales. He was imaginary.

Sometimes I was The Mexie or he was me, if you like, slipping so deftly into my body that bystanders never noticed, except for my puzzling lapses into broken English. At other times he simply rode beside me, invisible on his invisible steed, while I loped in four-quarter time, playing the dual role of man and horse.

When my brother grew old enough to ride with us, he felt left out, so I invented an alter ego for him: Pablo Gonzales, Pedro's younger brother, not as brave or bright as Pedro (a cross small brothers must bear when their elders are making the rules) but a nice-enough fellow. The four of us rode together for years, and made southern Saskatchewan safe for settlement.

Homemade fun, falling somewhere between make-believe and sheer ingenuity, was the driving force in all our lives. At very least it made those lives bearable. At best it made every day a celebration.

I wanted a bicycle but could not amass the necessary $28.50 until I was sixteen. So, for eight years I pushed an old car tire all over the farm at a dead run, humping it ahead with the heel of my hand and feeling only sightly deprived. In the blink of an eye it became an Eaton's Glider two-wheeler or, depending on my needs that day, a 1935 Packard Super 8.

I wanted a Wild West cap pistol with leather belt, holster and dummy bullets. A carved cedar shingle stuck in my pocket did the trick. I hosted imaginary dinner parties, using stones of appropriate shape and color for roasts of beef, baked potatoes, marble cake and fried eggs. One average stone pile provided a nourishing meal for two hundred guests.

When my father held school board meetings in our house I convened similar gatherings in the chicken coop. The members of my board clucked obediently in docile rows along their roosts while I telephoned distant places for new school teachers, through a knothole in the wall. I was busy and happy in my make-believe world. Once some small visitors came to play. I ignored them and went on talking to walls and chickens. A generation later, distraught parents would have shipped me off to a shrink, or muttered while wringing their hands, "Don't disturb him, he's *expressing* himself." My father said, "PLAY WITH YOUR LITTLE FRIENDS!" and grudgingly I did, with no visible scars on my psyche.

Although content in my solitude, it was better when Larry joined in. Now softball was possible: one of us served as pitcher and entire outfield, the other represented the team at bat plus opposing catcher. Naturally one side stayed at bat for hours (mine, if I could coerce my brother into letting me have first turn) and the scores were astronomical. Being four years younger, he endured endless bullying but somehow kept a sunny disposition.

We played hockey, sometimes on frozen ponds buffed by the wind, so mirror-perfect that the first skate mark was sacrilege. Other times we flooded a miniscule rink scooped out of snow, lugging a hundred pails of water from the pump until our soaked pant legs froze to steel. One of us was the entire Toronto Maple Leafs team. Faster than a speeding bullet, we dissolved into Apps (center), Horner (defense) or Broda (goal), depending on where the puck happened to be at a given moment. The other brother simultaneously faded in and out of the bodies of six Rangers or Canadiens or Red Wings. In March we played off for the Stanley Cup.

Our mother was a genius at improvisation. She stitched bathing suits out of old sweaters and — although we rose up from the slimy sloughs with waterlogged woollens sagging to our ankles — we felt very chic. She showed us how to build toy wagons out of shoe boxes with empty sewing spools for wheels, and how to make paper cowboys with a few deft snips of the shears.

She wrote bedtime stories and songs, and made scrapbooks literally from scraps: odd pieces of colored fabric cut to page size, heavily starched and bound with heavy thread. I kept scrapbooks of bird pictures, hockey players, prairie flowers, Christmas cards and, of course, everything I wrote.

I was in love with words. We told stories together, read aloud to one another, and read privately together, all four burrowed in our favorite living room chairs with books. The music of words ran chiming through my head. Some of my happiest times were hearing my father read aloud Paul Gallico stories on long winter nights and, again, a summer of herding cows when I curled up in a grassy ditch every sleepy afternoon, one eye on Reddy, Whiteface and their knobby-kneed children, the other on my book.

The best Christmas present I ever had was a Simplex Model A typewriter — a tiny tin contraption with a dial on top. By twirling any number or letter on the dial and pressing it down on an inked pad, I could print two words a minute. Immediately I published a household newspaper: SIX KITTENS BORN, GREYNOSE DOING WELL. At ten I won the one-dollar first prize for a six-paragraph fictional epic, "Christmas at the Browns," published in the *Torchbearers' Magazine*, a Regina *Leader Post* Saturday supplement for young people. From then on (My

God! *Money* for writing down words!) I knew what I wanted to do with the rest of my life.

Hundreds of middle-aged men and women today remember that magazine as a landmark in their young lives. We were all lonely and longing to reach outside our shells. From kitchen tables, attics and barn lofts all over the West, we poured out spidery longhand letters, moralistic essays, nature poems and awful fiction. The blessed magazine printed our stuff for all the West to read, rating it "C" to "A" in an effort to raise the standard. Sometimes our writing *did* improve and some like me were set on a course for life. Several poets, a few magazine writers and at least one novelist got their start as "Torchies." For the others it was simply a happy workout for the imagination — the best of all possible reasons for the magazine's existence. But it died on the threshold of World War II, never to be reborn. Perhaps today it could never compete with television.

The grown-ups of our community made their entertainment too: sleigh rides, skating parties, ice-cream socials, whist drives, softball tournaments, dances, amateur theatricals. Rarely did a night out cost more than ten cents. For hours of pleasure at *no* cost, there was "rubbering": gently, oh-so-softly lifting the telephone receiver and listening to neighbors spill out their secrets on the party line.

Box socials were the only way a lovesick man might fritter away his year's savings in five minutes. On the appointed evening each woman brought a daintily festooned box lunch for auction, with her name hidden inside. The top male bidder won the box and the right to dine with her. Sometimes romance blossomed over the bologna sandwiches, sometimes heartburn, but always the ladies' auxiliary or the softball fund came up solvent.

The bidder's task was to guess which box belonged to which eligible girl, or ugly but superb cook. Rarely did a box sell for more than five dollars. But once my father, when still a bachelor, and Donald Walker became locked in mortal bidding for a box they thought belonged to the prettiest single girl in the room. They went mad. The price soared beyond reason. Other bidders fell by the wayside. Suddenly my father's rational self heard Jack Collins, Cavalier, shouting "Ninety dollars!" That was three months' wages for a hired hand, or enough groceries for six months, or the price of that year's entire flax crop. A sick feeling clutched his gut.

"NINE-ty!" chimed the jubilant auctioneer. "NINE-ty going once . . . NINE-ty going twice . . . NINE-ty going. . . ."

"A HUNDRED!" thundered Donald Walker. My father turned away with a splendid show of regret. Walker, his appetite fading fast, paid for the prize. It did *not* belong to the prettiest single girl in the room. Its owner was a happily married woman whose husband then shared the hundred-dollar lunch with Donald.

After every box social, every whist drive or ball game, came the dance. Always the dance, always the same. . . .

*The men fling chairs and school desks from the center of the room. The girls giggle into the cloakroom to rouge their cheeks, paint their lips with Djer-Kiss, dab Evening in Paris on their earlobes, and ruthlessly dissect the young men shifting nervously from foot to foot in the next room. Bulky mothers settle massively along the sidelines, eyes darting for incriminating gossip to be presented at tomorrow morning's hearings on the party line.*

*Butch Gwin steps forth with a fresh shave and white shirt, a star of tonight's event. As "caller" he will announce each dance and, during square dances, will sing such crucial lines as "SWING YER PARTNERS, CORNERS ALL" and "NOW THE FIRST BIG COUPLE GET OUT IN THE MIDDLE AND SHAKE YER BIG FEET TO KEEP TIME WITH THE FIDDLE."*

*Gruffly self-important, he peels paraffin wax in curling chips over the dry splintered floor. Small boys surge out to slide on it, the way small boys are always drawn like magnets to anything slippery. And soon the floor has a semblance of sheen.*

*The band — a fiddler or two, an organist, sometimes a guitarist — tunes up with a plunking of C-notes, screeching of chords, dusting of resin on horsehair bows. They play all night for fifty cents if they are lucky; during one lean season they played all winter for a necktie apiece in the spring.*

*In tune at last, the leader nods at Butch. He sucks a mighty breath: "EEEEEVEREEBODY TWO-STEP!" The sweet-sad violins wail the opening bars of "Redwing." Sometimes a strong untrained voice yodels in the manner of Wilf Carter. Feet stomp, windows rattle. Couples in their shabby best spin and whirl and laugh, forgetting debts and drought and hopelessness for a while. And the children, wrapped in blankets and stacked like cordwood in a room apart, sleep fitfully into the night.*

Sometimes, unannounced on a summer evening, big redheaded Uncle George arrived on holiday from his comfortable government job in Moose Jaw. This was entertainment of the highest order: a visit from Outside. He rolled up our drive in his late-model car, with his glamorous World War I limp and a cloud of cigar smoke.

My parents neither drank nor smoked. Some adults, I knew, nipped furtively at bottles behind barns or dance halls. But Uncle George casually uncapped beer and shared it with Aunt Verda in *broad daylight.* I waited for the Devil to reach from the cellar and grab their ankles. But *no* — they merely grew more jolly!

The house was hushed when Uncle George's laughter boomed back to Moose Jaw. I salvaged his cigar butts, hid them under the verandah and sniffed them sometimes, while dreaming of cities, riches and wickedness.

But only sometimes. We managed well enough without new cars, visitors or travel. We were so rarely apart that when my father went to Regina for a medical checkup every two or three years, the house was intolerably empty. He phoned home at night, over his two- or three-day stay, never mind the staggering fifty-cent Long Distance charge. He was lonely too.

We were knit together by little ordinary events of life that my parents somehow turned into special occasions. When Larry and I brought home "A" report cards he solemnly shook our hands and made us feel important. My mother found time to run footraces with us; I was twelve before I could beat her. Once a blizzard marooned us for three weeks and the coal-oil lamps ran dry. But with the stove door open and storytelling by dancing firelight every night, we had such fun we hated the storm to end.

In December Larry and I hollered-up-the-chimney. As instructed in *The Boys Own Annual,* but lacking a fireplace as prescribed, we took stations in front of the stove's open door, peered into the flames and hollered:

"Santa Claus up in the sky so bright,
"Santa Claus, hear what we ask tonight."

Then we rattled off our Christmas list, parents listening attentively at our elbows — the adult "witnesses" insisted on by the *Annual*. Next we threw packages of salt on the coals. If the flames turned green, the book said, it meant Santa got the message. They always *did* turn green and we got our presents (since our parents had prudently picked our brains and ordered from Timothy Eaton weeks before).

Hollering completed, we brought down the decorations from the attic: four rolls of red and green crepe paper to be looped and twisted into streamers along the living room ceiling; seven red paper bells that opened like accordions; and an imitation tree that lasted all through the thirties. Each year its same green branches with imitation red berries unfolded to receive the same four tinkling bells, the same four tin horns that actually tooted, the same four exotic birds with saucy whisks of tails and clips for feet, the ropes of tinsel gone yellow with age.

On Christmas Eve we tidied the living room and set out tea, a mince tart and a welcome note for the expected visitor. Stockings were hung from the bookcase with care — and a mitten for Jiggs the terrier. In the black hush of morning, even before the sparrows began gossiping in the eaves, my father threw more coal on the fire. Before the lamps were lit Larry and I, shivering wildly and only partly from the chill, trained a flashlight on the tree.

Once I found a red pedal-car there; another time, a rocking horse that always bucked me off; each year, a crisp, green, Yankee dollar bill from Uncle Dorlan in California. Often the gift was merely a twenty-five-cent book, a hockey stick or bob-skates.

We liked to spend the day at home, and to give the animals Christmas dinner first. We pumped water steaming out of the ground into subzero air,

and tried to make their meal special: extra wheat for
the chickens, choice scraps for dogs and cats, a carrot
for each horse and cow.

Our own dinner in early afternoon was a triumph
of the farm: roast chicken, mounds of creamy mashed
potatoes, carrots, peas, turnips, bread, butter, pie,
cake, cookies. Only the Japanese oranges, cheddar
cheese, walnuts and filberts were store-bought treats
— but *such* treats. One Christmas Eve my father drove
the sleigh eleven miles through a blizzard to bring
home those oranges.

Another year, he saw Butch wandering alone
outside his shack.

"Nobody should be alone at Christmas," he said.
"What do you think, Mother?" What did she think?
She would have fed every lonely man in Sas-
katchewan if her table were long enough.

Larry and I buckled on our overshoes and
aviators' helmets and sprinted over the hill. Butch
was gruffly delighted ("Well, don't mind if I do . . ."").
Soon he was with us, freshly shaved, his thatch of
gray-sprinkled hair watered and brushed, chuckling
wheezily and heaping his plate to heights that
warmed my mother's heart.

To me — impresario for the day — Butch was
Heaven-sent. I was staging an after-dinner concert
with a one-act play; Larry and I were playing four
roles and my mother the fifth, and we were desperate
for an audience — although my father and the dog
had promised to do their best. Butch not only
doubled the applause but once even dabbed at his
eyes, moved to tears, I thought, by superior acting —
although it could have been his sinuses

Everyone rose for the mandatory singing of the
National Anthem. Then a little evening snack that, in
most jurisdictions, would pass for a five-course meal.

Heads nodding, in spite of vows to never fall asleep. Bedtime prayers: "Dear Jesus please bless Mom and Dad and Larry and Jiggs and Greynose and Tabby and Butch and help me to be good amen."

And it was over. Except that Christmas — like the red paper bells, like the crepe-paper streamers, like so much of our homemade fun — was still shiny and good when we unpacked it for another year.

# 13

## Butter Down the Well

It seemed meet, right and our bounden duty — as the Anglican Book of Common Prayer put it — for Larry and me to deliver our bedtime prayers in the form of a verbal letter to God or His Chosen Son. We were well acquainted with Both.

My mother saw to it that we were baptized, confirmed and at church on summer Sundays (the only season when clergy ventured into the territory). I knew how Jesus looked, from my Bible-story book. I knew the Devil abided somewhere below the water line and was probably a Liberal. And I was confident that God lived, because my father — while claiming to not believe in Him — was always addressing Him by name.

My father found genuine pleasure in swearing, and gave his vocal chords a daily workout. He drew the line at sexual swearwords in the presence of women and children, but the Deity was fair game any time.

It distressed my mother. He kept his awful secret throughout their courtship although once, she remembered later, he burned a finger and turned away with a muffled choking sound. But after the wedding, while painfully building a kitchen cabinet — he was a highly unskilled carpenter — he bashed his thumb and the air turned blue with blasphemy. Mother paled.

"Jack," she begged, "I *wish* you wouldn't say those things."

"Floy!" he roared, "if I didn't say those things I'd burst a blood vessel!"

They reached a compromise: she found nothing profane in "bloody"; so, for run-of-the-mill swearing he found comfort in "bloody ass," "bloody idiot" and other variations in the genre. But for total relief nothing could beat taking the name of the Lord in vain.

He was more agnostic than atheist. When Wiwa Hill Anglican Church was in summer session, he willingly took us there, for he wanted my brother and me to make up our own minds about religion. Anyway, he liked the civilized Sunday ritual.

Right after breakfast he shaved with high ceremony: swirling his badger-hair brush in a Yardley's shaving cup, whetting his old-fashioned Autostrop razor on a wide leather strap, lathering his cheeks with a Michelangelo touch, then cutting slow, deliberate swaths through the foam with much contortion and grimacing. A noisy rinse, a *slap-slap-slap* of Aqua Velva; then, extending his face to the nearest son, "Feel *that!* Smooth as a baby's bum. . . ."

"*Jack!*" my mother always cried in mock indignation, because it was expected of her, whereupon he winked at us like a naughty boy.

Larry and I were meanwhile elbow-deep in Nugget polish, brushing a gloss on his and our Sunday shoes. We donned our only suits. Then my father marshalled us for the leisurely three-mile drive among barbed-wire fences and clouds of clicking grasshoppers; a clustering of other scrubbed and polished families outside the diminutive white church; a gallant tip of his hat to the ladies; then he proudly guided his own flock into one of the fourteen pews.

On hot mornings the male heads among us tended to nod during The Order For Morning Prayer. It seemed unfair after a hard week's work to come to church for self-flagellation, admitting to "our manifold sins and wickedness," to being "miserable offenders" and to having "done those things we ought not to have done, and there is no health in us."

We were at our best during hymns. When the foot-pumped organ wheezed into "The Old Rugged Cross," my father's clear tenor rang above all the rest. During prayers he sat stiff and unbowed. Years later when I was in Europe with the RCAF he bowed his head during Sunday radio prayers for servicemen abroad, but he never prayed for himself. Praying for eleventh-hour forgiveness offended his sense of fair play. And prayer, he pointed out when pressed, had not prevented a bullet from exploding the skull of his best friend beside him in the trenches of France.

But these ironclad beliefs did not diminish his affection for the Sunday School girls. In winter Larry and I kept abreast of the faith with Sunday School correspondence courses. In summer the church's touring representatives came out to check up on us. One year a cloudburst mired their van in our gumbo roads — proving, I thought, that God sometimes *did* pour upon us the continual dew of His blessing, just as it claimed in Morning Prayer. Because the rain brought us, for two days, two lively, pretty college girls, Betty and Midge. Long enough for me to fall in love with Midge (she was seven years older and I never saw her again) and for my father to find new hope for the Anglican church.

He was equally cordial with the ministers who artfully fitted their house calls to mealtime. The literate Reverend Bowles and gregarious Reverend Brownlee were among his closest friends. They shrewdly avoided off-the-cuff sermons and found my father eager for intellectual arguments about books, politics, morality — about anything but doctrinaire religion.

Others were less perceptive. One morning just before noon the Reverend Rees came calling. A gentle, windy old man in the twilight of his career, his mind dwelt more in Heaven than on earth. Theology was his long suit; brevity was not. We planned to go to Gravelbourg that day, a thirty-three-mile round trip requiring only sightly less time and staging than the search for the Northwest Passage.

"Good thing you came this early or you'd have missed us," my dad said pointedly. "Because we're going to Gravelbourg. Right after a *quick* dinner."

Rev. Rees, already revving up for grace, neither heard nor cared. He blessed the food, at length. He relished the canned chicken that my mother hastily substituted for meat loaf. We finished the apple pie with whipped cream, called up from the reserve team in place of apple sauce, and began to rise. Rev. Rees raised a hand, his face suffused with radiance.

"LET US PRAY!" he cried.

Startled, we sank back. Nobody ever prayed *after* a meal. My mother, brother and I bowed our heads, sneaking a glance at my father. He sat bolt upright, with the clenched jaw reserved for welfare bums, enemies of the British Empire, and James G. Gardiner, Liberal minister of agriculture. Rev. Rees prayed long and fervently, oblivious to everything at ground level.

"Amen," he said at last.

"AMEN!" echoed Mother heartily, reading the storm signals across the table. We rose again.

"And now a hymn, friends!" cried Rev. Rees. " 'Rock of Ages!' ALL TOGETHER!"

There was not, of course, even a pitch pipe to set the key. Rev Rees's quavering voice searched in vain for the high notes. My mother stumbled in pursuit. Larry and I droned without moving our lips. My father stood silent with murder in his eyes. At last, with final blessing, Rev. Rees's beatific smile and silver head receded down the driveway. It was too late to go to Gravelbourg. My father stomped out to the barn, taking the Lord's name in vain.

All the same, he knew his Scriptures and leaned on them in time of stress. One summer day he was lowering four pounds of fresh butter into our version of a refrigerator — a cool, unused well. The rope, like so many other things on our farm, was frayed with age and overuse. It broke, and the butter fell sixty feet, totally beyond recall. Trivial, yes. But it was also symbolic of all those nerve-grating years: a man worked his guts out to the verge of some small triumph, then Fate or worn equipment snatched success away. Ordinary cursing was inadequate at such a time. Loud and clear like a furious benediction from Heaven itself, my father's sarcastic voice thundered over the plains: "THE LORD *GIVETH* . . . AND THE LORD *TAKETH AWAY* . . . ! *BLESSED* . . . BE THE NAME OF THE LORD!"

Hours later when he cooled off, we dared to laugh, and he joined in. There was comfort, we all agreed, to be found in one's faith.

# 14
## Standon School

There was only one serious flaw in my character, as I saw it. I *liked* school. It was a grievous handicap, and I never admitted to it publicly. Bad enough to score 90 in spelling and have tough semiliterate boys eye me thoughtfully as though measuring my pelt for the government bounty. So, every recess, I led the mandatory bitching about and bad-mouthing of teachers, long division, the history of England, the whole despicable education system. And secretly I welcomed the mile-and-a-half ramble through pasture and rutted roads to Standon School.

Standon stood on its own stark, grassy yard, its white paint peeling and not one tree to relieve the barren landscape. Its lone classroom held twenty-five desks for grades one to ten. There were two miniscule cloakrooms and a "library" — two bookshelves in a cubicle beside the coal bin. Nearby stood a two-room "teacherage," the girls' privy, a well with a bucket on a rope and — as far removed as possible — the animals' facilities: horse barn and boys' privy.

From our doorstop this tantalizing scene was in full view, and its lack of aesthetics mattered not one iota to me. Long before the enrollment age of six, I yearned to be there. My mother had taught me to read. I raced through my storybooks and longed for new words to conquer. From the first day of school — where I went immaculate in shirt, tie, polished shoes and short trousers, and later arrived home rumpled, sweaty, with a black eye and demanding to wear denim bib-overalls like other boys — I revelled in it.

School was books. School was where you won spelling matches, got "A"s in composition and sometimes, modestly ducking your head, heard the teacher read aloud a particularly eloquent piece of your work. School was where you mastered the vital rural art of blowing your nose without a handkerchief: delicately pressing each nostril, overhand with thumb or forefinger, and blasting toward the ground, taking care to lean away from your trousers, your friends and the prevailing wind.

School was a riot of smells: wet overalls steaming dry in front of the furnace after you fell in the pond at recess; a whiff of urine from the girl two rows over who was cursed with weak kidneys; chalk dust billowing as you cleaned the felt-padded blackboard erasers by pounding them on the outside wall; fragrant, oiled Dust-Bane, spread on the floor before sweeping; the knockout aroma of Spanish onion sandwiches when kids untinned their syrup-pail lunch boxes.

School was going home in spring among flooded ruts, building mud dams, launching homemade boats and arriving late and gloriously sheathed in gumbo to a mother's wrath. School was where on rainy recesses the big boys commanded us little ones, "C'mon down t' the shithouse fer a smoke."

Tingling with wickedness we crowded into the foul-smelling two-holer, sneaking backward glances for the teacher whose eyes, like God's, were ever on us. Somebody lit up a twist of toilet paper, coarse, gray, smouldering stuff. We took drags in turn, gagging, spitting, eyes watering, trying to be debonair, until we tumbled back to class, redolent as smoked herring. Our teacher, Miss Dempson, must surely have sniffed out our secret but she was tolerant. We knew *she* smoked *real* cigarettes in her teacherage at lunch hour. This — at a time when teachers were never to smoke, neither drink, neither covet their neighbors' husbands — made her the Germaine Greer of her generation.

School began at nine with the clang of her hand-held bell. We lined up beside our desks, droning through the National Anthem and "Our-FatherwhoartinHeaven . . . ," with eyes fixed glassily on faded prints of Millet's *Angelus* and His Gracious Majesty King George.

Then, depending on the day and the teacher's whim, we raised our fingernails for inspection and lied about whether we had brushed our teeth, drunk eight glasses of water and slept for eight hours. So much for the subject known as Health.

If it was winter our health then went rapidly downhill. The black, hulking coal furnace in the corner never hit its stride until noon. Subzero winds sifted under the ill-fitting door. We huddled in double-knit sweaters, feet like blocks of ice, noses always clogged, mouths stained black from Smith Brothers cough drops, hacking and sneezing in a cacophony of misery. By afternoon the furnace was in fine fettle. We sat stupefied in our Penman's drop-seat underwear, sluggishly hanging on until three thirty when the teacher called "Dismissed!"

Yet we learned as much as any pupils any time. Jean Dempson instilled in me more English literature and grammar than any high school or university thereafter. For her it was a labor of love: theoretically, her salary was five hundred dollars a year but the school board never had that much. She was paid ten dollars a month plus weekly gifts of farm produce.

Nevertheless it was a job — and for her *more* than just a job — and she stuck with us for six and a half years. She was part of the continuity and security of school. Our personal friendships and enmities endured even longer because, for ten years, we never left that room. Upon promotion to a higher grade we simply moved into the row of next-larger desks. Boys and girls played all the games together; the best softball catcher we ever had was named Gladys. School was our second family.

But it was no mealy-mouthed Dick-and-Jane kind of school. It was rough. Gladys the catcher never owned a mask and rarely a glove. Outfielders' gloves were unheard of, and the lumpy ball diamond put weird hops on grounders, leaving our fingers warped like pretzels. There were fist fights, preceded by baleful threats of "Ya better watch it, I'm really gonna fix yer wagon this time."

There was a game called "stick," like field hockey except the puck was a battered tin can with jagged edges. We clubbed it among our unprotected bodies until the whole enrollment had battered toes and damaged knees. In the game of "horse" two small boys mounted two big boys' shoulders and wrestled it out until one was dumped headfirst on the iron turf. At very least our necks were pulled like taffy; at worst we suffered mild concussion.

On winter mornings when we arrived with beet-red faces and dripping noses, older boys seized and "warmed" our ears, rubbing them violently until our brains rattled. Sometimes the ranking big boy hoisted me by my head (a form of sport called "seeing London," because the pressure on the temples momentarily blacked you out). Another offered "Wanna see the moon?" and when some ever-gullible junior stared up an empty coat sleeve as invited, his elder dumped a cup of water in his eyes. Sometimes the head bully demonstrated how a certain small boy had been trained to weep instantly on command.

"Bawl! Stop!" the bully cried proudly, turning his victim on and off like a faucet.

Miss Dempson herself was rated "tough" by the class. She had to be. Several boys towered over her, restlessly attending school by parental edict until they reached dropout age. She controlled them with sheer will and the threat of her ultimate weapon, the strap. It was the H-bomb of its time, a massive deterrent: black harness leather a foot long, two inches wide and a half-inch thick. She rarely even pulled it from her drawer.

All day we were around her, straining her nerves, testing her patience, invading her space. In fair weather we played "anti-eye-over," throwing a ball interminably back and forth over her roof — *bump-trickle-bounce* — until it fell down her chimney and stunk up her premises with burnt rubber. On stormy days we huddled indoors at recess, wrestling, flipping pocketknives into the splintery floor and pestering the girls. The easiest way to start a fight was to point out a victim, twirl a forefinger meaningfully against one's forehead and sneer, "Lookit, she jist got outa *Weyburn!*" Weyburn, being southern Saskatchewan's site of a mental hospital, was synonymous with crazy.

Sometimes when the teacher's back was turned Walter Bell, the born adventurer among us, tossed .22 shells into the glowing furnace to see if they were, indeed, "Dangerous Within A Mile" as the ammunition box said. His delight, when they exploded, was touching. Luckily the stove was of cast iron surrounded by a sheet metal shell, or the flower of Standon's young manhood would have been wiped out in a single recess.

Miss Dempson's punishment was swift, fair and geared to the crime. For inattention to lessons or routine stupidity the culprit stayed after school writing a hundred lines on the blackboard ("I will not talk in class" was a perennial). Passing illicit notes, blasting a classmate with spitballs from a rubber band, or farting with deliberate intent to disrupt the class was handled with a searing look, a sharp word or a rap on the knuckles. Repeat offenders were sent to stand facing the corner. My friend Gilbert was sometimes led there by one glowing red ear.

In fact, because we *were* promptly punished, we behaved reasonably well. Rare was the child who talked back to a teacher; we knew if she couldn't handle us our parents would. Strappings at home were common, and there wasn't a spoiled child among us. It allowed teachers to get on with teaching, and making school a pleasant social experience.

On that latter count, we contributed as much as she did. We had absolutely no school board funds for games, equipment, social outings or fetes. We earned or invented it all. Every February 14, for instance, the school valentine box, a carton covered with pink crepe paper and red hearts, received our homemade love/hate offerings to one another. Year after year Larry and I stockpiled colored paper, string, ribbon and tinfoil, and racked our brains for fresh inventions. We pasted little hearts over bigger hearts over biggest hearts; tinfoil arrows piercing red paper hearts; hearts with frilly edging made from perforated linings of candy boxes; hearts with scalloped edges; hearts with handprinted sentiments ("Dearest little friend of mine/Will you be my Valentine?"); and valentines with boy-girl magazine pictures, usually the Campbell's Soup Kids. When the Depression ended and everyone bought Eaton's catalogue valentines we felt bereft.

Every school had a free Christmas concert. Ours drew audiences from a dozen miles around because Jean Dempson was uncommonly musical, literate and a born impresario. Her specialty was costume numbers. Our Biblical wise men were impeccably turned out in striped pyjamas and tea-towel burnooses. Shepherds watched their flocks in bed sheets, toting papier-mâché crooks. Once we built a stunning Bethlehem stable, big enough for Joseph and Mary to stand up in, from dried, matted Russian thistle.

Our mothers worked with bloodshot eyes, sewing far into the nights by kerosene light, turning scraps into clever outfits for platoons of brownies and elves. At times they must have questioned the sense of it. Once Gilbert and I rustled on stage as twin Christmas trees. We were a vision of pastoral loveliness in green and brown crepe paper. Our mothers had worked a week on those costumes. We were on view for precisely four minutes.

Yet how could the mothers refuse? The concert was such pleasure for all of us. From October to mid-December we gladly gave up our recesses and after-school hours to rehearse. Nobody was left out. Those too shy or lacking in talent to sing a song or recite a poem could always march in a musical drill. For weeks Miss Dempson coaxed and harangued and jollied us, and made us seem better than we were. . . .

*It is concert night at last. We are drilled to nervous perfection, and our mothers are ready to faint. Up goes a tiny stage of raw planks, and a curtain on a rope. As the crowd arrives we peer through the slits, old troupers sizing up the house.*

*Thirty, forty, maybe fifty people squeeze into the room in wrinkled Sunday dresses, Botany Serge suits, sheepskin coats and Piss Pot hats. How strange all those expectant friends and neighbors look in the white, hissing light of the gasoline lamps.*

*As always, we begin with "O Canada." Auntie May Walker, hunched at the organ, hits most of the right notes. My father, as secretary of the school board, announces the program. There are carols, with good singers ranged in front and the tin ears hidden in the back. There are plays and poems recited in self-conscious monotones. Roy Bien plays the guitar and yodels. Thunderous applause. Little Walter Pouteaux, grinning engagingly beneath an enormous cowboy hat, shouts out "When It's Roundup Time in Texas and the Bloom Is on the Sage." The crowd goes wild.*

*There is a musical drill, "March of the Wooden Soldiers." Mac Smart, swinging his arms vigorously as a good wooden soldier should, suddenly feels his crepe-paper pants falling down. He grabs them and keeps marching; the crowd sniggers but applauds his guts.*

*Now I'm on for a solo as Little Jack Frost. My mother has surpassed herself: composed music and lyrics, and contrived a costume of white crepe paper, cotton batting, artificial snow, conical hat and assorted pieces of old bedsheet.*

*I step out glittering whitely and walking stiffly so as not to split my paper pants. The audience breathes an admiring "ahhh!" Afterward, in the spirit of Christmas, the big boys refrain from beating me up, although sorely tempted by my sweet, white long stockings.*

*For two happy hours, the tiny room expands to contain the heat, lights, laughter, handclaps and reedy voices issuing from the planks. Who needs Broadway when you have a Standon Christmas concert . . . ?*

We did everything that way, with scraps and gusto. Nothing was impossible, we were sure of it. This feeling of invincibility led to the events of June 1939. Our new teacher, Catherine MacKenzie, all energy and ambition, announced we would enter the track-and-field meet at Bateman, ten miles distant. We had to ask what track and field *was*, but her enthusiasm was infectious. We dug pits, raised hurdles, raced and jumped every recess and evening for a month. Our speeds and distances improved. We were good, no doubt about it. Maybe good enough to win the silver trophy.

The day of the meet dawned gray and wet. Wally James, an amiable bachelor who had a crush on the teacher, brought his truck. All seventeen of us climbed in, blue-denimed aristocrats off to the guillotine. My father was mending a fence as we drove by. Naturally *he* was a believer. "Bring back that trophy!" he roared. We waved jauntily.

Bateman — awesome enough any time with its four-room school and population of two hundred — was crowded with confident athletes from miles around. *They* knew what track and field meant. They wore track shorts. They wore track *shoes!* We watched incredulously as they high-jumped from an angle, rolling gracefully over the bar. Our tactic was to charge it head-on. (Eureka! *That* was why we always nose-dived in the dirt!) We finished fifth in fields of five. By noon we were the joke of the meet: when a Standon competitor stepped forth the others broke into fits of laughter.

We huddled wet and wretched over lunch. The indefatigable Walter Bell led us to a local grain elevator, a guided tour designed to lift our spirits. In clambering around the place, he tore his pants so badly on a nail that we had to form a human screen and piece him together with safety pins. It was that kind of day. Any fool could see it would only go downhill from there. We wanted to go home.

"It doesn't matter if you lose," Miss MacKenzie pleaded. "Just try. Show them we're good sports."

Being a good sport seemed a lot less fun than winning, but we stayed. We finished with three points. Waves of laughter rose as our score was bellowed over the public address system. Silently we climbed in our rain-soaked truck.

The sun came out. After a few miles, with hateful Bateman behind us, somebody broke into the current hit song, "Doing the Lambeth Walk." Everybody sang. Our senses of humor seeped back. By the time we debarked at dear, familiar Standon School it didn't hurt so much.

"What do we owe you for the day and your gas?" asked Miss MacKenzie.

"Would two dollars be too much?" said Wally James.

We each produced a dime. The teacher made up the extra thirty cents. We went home battle-scarred but healing. We had learned how to lose, a lesson infinitely more valuable than the square root of the hypotenuse. It was a lesson we'd all have a chance to use again.

# 15

## The Night the King Came to Moose Jaw

In most respects the spring of 1939 was like all the rest, a tantalizing mixture of hope and despair. Redwing blackbirds shrilled from the slough-bottoms. Gophers with insouciant smiles popped up from their holes like small, furry periscopes. But May came in hot and dry, withering the fragile shoots of wheat. Grasshopper eggs hatched quickly in the sun, threatening yet another plague that would strip the fields of every living thing. The horse-killing disease, encephalomyelitis, was going the rounds again. Another Bad Year in the making.

Then one morning the news raced along the party line: "The King and Queen are coming to Canada!" A shock wave of pure delight ran behind it. Never before had a reigning British monarch set foot on one of the "dominions."

To most of us in those simpler times, kings and queens were holy figures, and none more than

George VI and Elizabeth. The timing was perfect. The world was on the brink of war. Canada was staggering into its tenth year of Depression, an endless round of dust, drought and breadlines. Now, right out of a fairy tale, Their Gracious Majesties were coming to lighten our dreary days. And nowhere was George VI more revered than in our house.

My father was as loyal a subject as the Empire ever had. When the National Anthem played he stood rigidly at attention and expected everyone around him to do the same. Once in the Shamrock community hall during "God Save the King" I saw him freeze a gaggle of sniggering teenagers with one furious glance. In the early 1940s when we finally owned a radio, the Anthem once caught us at bedtime. Instantly my dad sprang to his feet, ramrod straight, in his long johns.

So we rejoiced in the Royal Visit, even though we would never see Their Gracious Majesties. They would cross Canada by train but their nearest stop, on May 25, would be Moose Jaw, sixty miles away. Return fare for the four of us was about ten dollars — food and clothing for a month. Moose Jaw might as well have been the moon.

We had no radio. The Regina *Leader Post* was still our only lifeline to the world. George VI, the *Leader* said, was packing most of his fifty uniforms for the long journey. Small communities across Canada were planting trees and scrubbing down city halls for the occasion. The Imperial Order, Daughters of the Empire was sponsoring an essay contest: "Why I wish to be in Moose Jaw on May 25." An entire Ottawa school was getting long recesses so the children could line the street, wave flags and cheer, to help the nervous horses of the Royal Canadian Dragoons get used to crowds. The world-famous Dionne quintuplets, not yet five years old, were going to Toronto for a special audience with the royal couple.

My father wistfully studied the *Leader Post*. As usual, our sole cash income was his pension, fifteen dollars a month. Still, fifteen dollars *would* cover the trip to Moose Jaw. . . .

On Saturday, May 6, the King and Queen boarded the *Empress of Australia* for Canada. On Sunday the year's first dust storm swirled across the fields. It was mild compared to the one that struck on May 9. That day, a forty-mile-an-hour wind lifted the topsoil and blacked out southern Saskatchewan. As usual, sand seeped around doors, under windowsills, onto tables, floors, dishes, clothes, and as usual, lamps were lit at noon. Cars stopped, with visibility down to zero, and at Parkbeg on the nearby CPR main line a train had to wait for the air to clear. Most of the little wheat plants clung stubbornly to the fields, but we knew the next storm might wipe out them and our hopes for another year. And my father knew he'd need that fifteen dollars.

Now the Royal Visit crowded everything off the front pages. The *Leader Post* instructed readers to address the King as "Sir" and the Queen as "Ma'am," should we happen to meet them. We read that grandstand seats along the royal route in Toronto were selling for five dollars each, and silently hated Toronto a little more.

On the morning of May 17 the *Empress of Australia* docked at Quebec City, in sight of the Plains of Abraham. "THUNDERING CHEERS ECHO ALONG CLIFFS," screamed the *Leader Post*. My father was in Shamrock that day, and came home with the grim look of a man about to slay a dragon.

"Mother," he said, "the boys *have* to see this. We're *going*, come hell or high water!"

I can only guess at how they must have weighed and worried that enormous decision far into the night.

"How can we leave the baby chicks? They're only two weeks old!" she said. "And the cows have to be milked at night. No, you three go, I'll stay and look after the place."

"The chickens will be all right," Dad said firmly. "The cows can wait till morning. We're all going." And it was settled.

If I had ever doubted the power of the King, not any more. I was fourteen but I had never been to Moose Jaw, nor ridden a train. We never left the cows unmilked. And those 250 baby chickens were a vital part of our 1939 food and income strategy.

But we were going. And now we dared to wallow with the rest of Canada in a royalty-worshipping binge. The blue and gold twelve-car train sped west through waves of adulation: "MONTREALERS CRAM THE STREETS"; "A MILLION TORON-TONIANS CHEER THEM." From Ottawa the *Leader Post* correspondent revealed that the King had "a real man's voice, warm and cordial. . . . His tanned skin, clear eyes and strong handgrip tell a story of health and clean living." And the Queen? "The camera misses her inner light . . . quite like someone out of a fairy tale . . . you expect her to dissolve in thin air at any moment. . . ."

On the weekend, God threw in a bonus — two inches of glorious, life-giving rain, and more came early in the week. Thursday, May 25, dawned clear and muddy. We rose early and gave the animals enough food for twenty-four hours. The dirt roads were a mess but we hitched up a team and wagon, pulled coats over our Sunday-best clothes and drove to Shamrock, the wheels flinging showers of mud around us.

The 10 A.M. train chuffed in late as usual, and already half-full of patriots from all along the branch line. We settled on hard wicker seats. The coach smelled deliciously of age and cinders. The whistle sent a great mourning wail echoing off the grain elevators and the train lunged forward. We were off to Moose Jaw to see the King.

Mother had packed a huge basket of ham sandwiches and cookies to see us through lunch and supper. But the excitement and hunger were contagious. Everyone else was eating and we ate too, demolishing every crumb.

We reached Moose Jaw in mid-afternoon. Was there any city so big, so magnificent? Some of the buildings were four, maybe five storeys high. Its normal population of twenty thousand had merely doubled that day, but it might as well have been a half million. Outside the railway station a squad of Mounties maneuvered in full-dress uniform. For ten years I had read "King of the Royal Mounted"; I knew "Sergeant Silk the Prairie Scout" by heart; but I had never seen a live Mountie *in scarlet*. If the squad had trampled me on the spot, I would have died with a smile.

We passed a little platform where local dignitaries would meet Their Gracious Majesties that night about nine thirty. The crowds swept us along Main Street. Then, as now, it ran arrow-straight from the station through the heart of Moose Jaw. All the action was here — Union Jacks, Red Ensigns and multi-colored bunting fluttered from every lamp post; great floodlights hung ready for the evening; an enormous electric organ stood on the sidewalk to entertain the crowds and serenade the royal visitors.

At five o'clock my father fought his way into a restaurant to buy soft drinks and doughy sandwiches at outrageous prices. Already wooden barricades were going up to shield store windows from the billowing crowds. Dad found us places near the curb, then marched away with a thousand other veterans to get an armband and beret, line the parade route and form an honor guard for his King.

All through that long, long evening it rained and our Sunday finery sagged. Moose Jaw did its best to entertain us. The organ played, bands marched, Mounties pranced on matching bay horses, girl guides and scouts trooped by, Moose Jaw's school children paraded and then — disaster — hundreds of them took up positions in front of us. It was nearly nine thirty.

Then a kind school principal looked back, saw us and beckoned. "Go! Hurry!" cried my mother. We boys squeezed in among the school children.

"The Royal Train has arrived," boomed a loud-speaker. We peered down the street, hardly daring to breathe. Somewhere on that platform the local aldermen and their wives were having their moment with royalty. Finally the screams: "THEY'RE COM-ING!" The din turned into one long, hoarse roar. Leaning far out, I glimpsed my father, standing so straight I feared he would never bend again.

The motorcade came, but moving too fast for the aldermen had used up too much time. I glimpsed a dark, smiling woman and a serious man in a peaked military cap. Behind in a second car, as consolation prize, was Prime Minister Mackenzie King. In a flash they were gone.

The King and Queen drove eight blocks up Main Street that night and hurried back to their train to stay on schedule. Their allotted time in Moose Jaw was exactly thirty minutes. My mother never saw their faces, although she said the Queen had a lovely hat.

We elbowed our way toward the station, dazed with fatigue and excitement. Moose Jaw set off fireworks, prepared Main Street for an outdoor dance, and opened a midway. But the midway events were five cents each, which we couldn't afford. Anyway, it was time to go home. At one in the morning our train crept slowly into the country. We boys stayed up all night, prowling the aisles, drinking the water cooler dry and unwinding from the miracle of the day.

At dawn we reached Shamrock, hitched up our horses, and drove home through the dew, the clean wet earth and the blessed prairie silence. A huge red sun climbed in the east. Our waiting animals eyed us reproachfully. We fed them, filled ourselves with bacon and eggs, and tumbled into bed. We did not feel cheated that we had seen so little. We had seen so *much*.

For my dad was right when he scrimped and sacrificed to shepherd us to Moose Jaw that day. It was one of those moments in a lifetime when logic is illogical. He gave us a glimpse not just of a king but of the world. It was fifteen dollars well spent.

# 16

## A Three-Letter Word Called "Shh!"

On my father's fifty-ninth birthday I gave him a copy of the current best-seller, *For Whom the Bell Tolls*. Hemingway was his kind of writer — macho deeds, gritty prose — but he warned me away from the book.

"It's not for little boys to read," he said enigmatically.

Instantly my pulse quickened. I wasn't as little as he thought. Obviously *For Whom the Bell Tolls* contained explicit sex — rare in my reading and essential to my education.

The moment my father left the house I was reading it, hidden inside a copy of the *Saturday Evening Post*. But apart from reporting that "the earth moved" during the sex act — which seemed geologically impossible — Hemingway told me what I already knew. Nothing.

Like every growing boy anytime, anyplace, I spent

nine-tenths of my day thinking about sex. Unlike modern adolescents, I was an ignoramus. There was no *Joy of Sex*, no *Penthouse* with four-color graphics, no liberated women uttering four-letter specifics. Hemingway's oblique description of love in a sleeping bag was the raciest stuff in print. In the movies, Nelson Eddy and Jeanette MacDonald mostly held hands. Around the neighborhood, if a boy got a girl "in trouble" he was quick-marched to the altar with a grim platoon of her relatives in lockstep behind him, before I (or he) knew exactly what happened.

My parents, like all others, never discussed the forbidden subject in our presence. "Shh!" they warned, whenever it threatened to come up. But they couldn't completely shield us from sex because the fields and barnyards were full of it. Roosters were constantly ravaging the hens. Cows were calving like clockwork. Cats were bearing new litters of kittens as fast as the next itinerant tom came humming and strumming down the road. Lust-crazed dogs were forever sexually assaulting the legs of unwary strangers. And each summer I served as panderer for the pumpkins. Pumpkins must be cross-fertilized and, since we were short of bees along with everything else, I had to dust pollen from the male flower into the female if I wanted jack-o-lanterns.

As manhood approached I was accorded the honor of watching the cow "get serviced." Maybe my parents were trying to tell me something. When Whiteface XIV or Old Reddy XXI showed signs of heat, my father hastily tied her behind the wagon and led her down-road to a man who owned a bull. The bull — a jaded old swordsman, with an air of perpetual ennui — rose up wearily, sniffed her nether regions, mounted her, then rudely turned his back and ate grass. No fore- or after-play for *his* cows. But the bull owner — much the way Foster Hewitt made hockey games seem better than they really were — provided a color commentary: "Lookit, lookit! Chee-zuz! He's really goin' to town now!" Then we paid our two dollars and, if the bull was any kind of a man, led home a satisfied and pregnant Old Reddy.

Even amidst all these febrile goings-on I had only the haziest notion of how *people* went about sex. At age six I found in an old trunk a book on feminine hygiene entitled *Herself*, which told me nothing I wanted to know and a lot of things I didn't. There was the corset section of Eaton's catalogue, of course — the prairie lad's *Playboy*, page after page of sexless Amazons with billowing bosoms and bovine faces, all armor-clad in whalebone and elastic. Sometimes, fixing me with their idiotic half smiles, they coyly turned up a corner of corset to reveal the sturdy merchandise — but nothing else. On many a languorous winter afternoon I sat under the dining room table, catalogue in sweaty palms, trying to fathom the Mystery of the Half-Turned Corset.

School educated me in ways my parents wouldn't have dreamed. Naturally the boys told dirty jokes incessantly, and bragged of sexual conquests that were biologically impossible. Two had reputedly done (at age eight) unspeakable things to a girl in the library (that miserable thin-walled cubicle next to the coal bin). But even the erotic *lie* was a dazzling new vista to me.

Walking home from school, my friends and I swapped dirty jokes. When the supply ran low we invented more. Eager for their approval I set out at age six to establish myself as a new talent. We were booting pebbles downhill one May afternoon when a fellow traveller absently tossed out a couplet:

"Let a fart
"And then you'll start . . ."

Trigger-fast I shot back:

"Let 'er blow
"And awaaay you'll go."

It was not exactly Ogden Nash but we were convulsed by our wit. My friends looked at me with new respect — maybe there was hope after all for this little bugger with his short pants and clean shirts — and turned to serious tutelage. From then on, every afternoon, we majored in Pornography I. We never dallied because, as one brother warned his juniors,"You don't come straight home from school and get behind a team of horses, the Ole Man's gonna kick your ass all the way to Shamrock!" But you can tell a lot of dirty jokes in a mile and by grade two I had assembled a vague image of boys-and-girls-together.

Crude drawings like the works of Stone Age man, on the walls of the boys' john, were explicit but the sticklike figures didn't seem to be having much fun. In the school barn I watched and listened as big boys whiled away rainy recesses measuring their penises with a foot ruler — a micrometer would have done the trick — or swapping sex legends. One local bachelor, the story went, was endowed with an organ so large that women fled from its sight and he was forced to bestow his favors on cattle. At each retelling our little eyes grew rounder with revulsion and respect.

Sometimes we discussed whores (pronounced "hoo-ers"). None of us had ever seen a hoo-er but we guessed she had moist scarlet lips, rippling buttocks and heroic breasts. Breasts loomed larger in our fantasies than in our neighborhood.

Sometimes, in the teasing games at recess, older kids arbitrarily paired small boys with small girls, snickering innuendos and holding us close together while we kicked and screamed with outrage. It did nothing for me. The girls were spare, angular little creatures. I wanted an older woman and at age ten found her. She was fourteen, a slim ethereal blonde, a *Torchbearers'* poet and a nature lover like me. I never bared my feelings but I think she enjoyed my cow-eyed devotion.

Mostly I loved her mind, although her body began to look better by the day. We met regularly at school but rarely talked — the teasing would have been brutal. We passed notes via her disgusted younger brother. If he steamed them open, as any right-thinking brother should have, he found a purely intellectual affair. The letters were always signed "Sincerely" and dwelt on the latest *Torchbearers'* activities.

We moved on to a more intimate ritual: "taking yer hat." At recess she snatched the cap from my head and I tried to get it back or vice versa. Properly managed, the game involved a lot of clutching and grabbing under the guise of clean fun, and the excitement nearly made me swoon.

Then a fifteen-year-old fell in love with her too (because, I told myself darkly, I had turned her into a woman). One morning as I wrested the tam from her golden curls the big boy dealt me out. He lifted the tam and me and with three violent shakes, the way terriers kill rats, took away the prize. The blonde, giggling with delight, turned in pursuit. I slunk away and thought of joining the Foreign Legion.

I began going to country dances, a special kind of masochism. I was psychologically incapable of dancing. I loved music, my parents were excellent dancers, but out on the floor my joints automatically locked. My mother tried to teach me, propelling my wooden body around the living room until we sank from exhaustion. I sent away for a mail-order course, cut out the set of paper footsteps that arrived, and followed their bewildering path across the floor without music: Uh-one-two-three-one-two-three. It never worked.

Yet staying home was far worse, for the next day friends would smirk, "Din't see ya at the dance. S'matter, ya sick or somethin'?" — knowing, of course, that my only ailment was cowardice.

So invariably I showed up on the sidelines in my old but snappy blue serge suit (Eaton's advertised everything as "snappy") and my best Douglas Fairbanks expression: an animated flash of teeth, an amused tilt of eyebrows toward the dance floor. My friend Roy Bien would be dancing, wearing the newest-style Eaton's suit (vest with lapels). He was getting better looking every day and had, in the parlance of the times, a "good line with girls." Over beside the furnace, I feigned urgent conversation with old women and felt my acne grow.

When the act became unbearable I stretched my aching cheeks in one last jaunty grin and sauntered to the cloakroom. It was full of other losers, comrades in misery. We had seen each other at school that very day but now we exchanged loud startled cries and witty repartee: "Cold enough fer ya?," "How's yer belly fer spots?" or "Jist get in from Weyburn? Haw!" We arm-wrestled, talked about hoo-ers and tried to ignore the seductive sob of violins and the tinkle of female laughter. Finally, if God had any mercy, it was midnight, late enough to go home without losing face.

I fell in love again. She was small, winsome, bursting with personality — and more. She had a *shape*. Other girls in my age group were still built like posts but this girl was a veritable Eaton's catalogue Junior Miss.

Our affair began with another contemporary mating rite — "tapped ya last" — basically tag, but with a more affectionate touch than the vicious straight-arm that normally went with that game. We held hands furtively during recesses or school concerts. We invented flirtation by song titles. Other kids thought we were exchanging insults. Only a keen student of current pop songs could recognize our language of love.

"Scatterbrain!" I muttered (from ". . . Nothing else can matter, you're my darling scatterbrain . . .").

"Little Sir Echo!" she murmured suggestively. (That song's last line was: ". . . But you're always so far away. . . .")

"Careless!" I panted. (". . . Careless, careless in everything you do. . . .")

I had just plucked up courage to accidentally brush my arm against her bosom when I graduated from grade ten — the end of the line in our country school.

I began commuting by bicycle and saddle horse to Shamrock High. World-weary and wise, I brought back tales of high life in the metropolis. In truth, I was shy, unathletic, a gawky scarecrow in my father's castoff shirts, and totally out of step with the wise-eyed village kids. I had never been more miserable.

Then she too graduated, to another district high school — and fitted into the new life as though born to it. Soon the bad news seeped back as fast as my friends could carry it: she was dating an air force pilot. *An air force pilot!* Worse yet, he was a good dancer! This was competition beyond my blackest nightmares. I began to realize how Joseph must have felt when he learned that Mary had been seeing the Holy Ghost. Still, if I could somehow improve my personality. . . .

I sold twenty-nine gopher tails and bought Dale Carnegie's *How To Win Friends and Influence People*. It urged me to smile incessantly and pay fulsome compliments. I leered into the mirror and exclaimed, as Dale advised, "My, what a lovely head of hair you have!" The apparition in the mirror looked back glumly from beneath its lank, greasy locks and said nothing.

It came my turn to join the air force. The night before I went away, the remnants of our old gang gathered at Standon School for a farewell party. My sometime love was there. I was no bargain — six feet tall and 123 pounds of solid bone and bad skin. But this was no time to think about the Fleischman's Yeast I should have eaten or the Charles Atlas body-building course I could have taken.

Swallowing my terror, I bared my teeth in the Dale Carnegie manner. "Gonna lemme see ya home tonight?"

"Sure."

We mounted our bicycles and rode up hill and down until we came to the last coulee before her farm.

"I'll be all right from here on," she said, meaning she didn't want me at her door. But wait! She could not brush off an air force man so easily. I closed in with grim resolve.

"Kiss ya goodbye?"

"Okay."

For years I had daydreamed this scenario. I was Robert Jordan, hero of *For Whom the Bell Tolls*. She was my lover, Maria. We were somewhere in Spain. . . .

*Her arms crept around my neck and tightened.*

*"I did not know thou cared for me!" she whispered. "I want to kiss thee better!"*

*"Nay, little rabbit!" I said. "Put thy arms around me and we shall feel the earth move. . . ."*

In fact, not much of anything moved out there on the dirt road south of Standon School. There was a brief, dry bashing of lips, her bicycle still between us. Then, with the lethal intuition of womankind, she said lightly, "First kiss?"

I was devastated. How in hell did she *know?* Luckily it was dark.

"Not quite," I lied airily and, with my best Douglas Fairbanks wave, pedalled away into the night, still virginal and burning with humiliation. Ah well, I was off to the air force where nobody would know or prejudge me. And I had finally kissed a girl. Now, *anything* could happen.

# 17

## Last Days

Shamrock — The Victory Boosters Tobacco League held a variety concert at Rouen School May 29. The president of the local chapter of the league, McGowan Smart, was master of ceremonies and chief director of the program.

Features of the evening were vocal numbers by Jean Lightbody, Mildred Miller, Larry Collins and Mrs. Radcliffe. Instrumental music was supplied by Kenneth and Bill Lightbody. George Marriott submitted two humorous selections. Pupils of Rouen School presented a very cleverly conducted puppet show and a quiz contest completed the evening's entertainment. The purpose of the concert was to provide cigarettes for Canadian troops overseas and was a definite success. A sum of $15.50 was collected.

Regina *Leader Post*, June 6, 1942.

I treasure that faded news clipping, not merely because I wrote it, as a *Leader* rural correspondent for ten cents an inch, but because it demonstrates how one small corner of Canada did its part in World War II. All over the land unimportant people like us were rallying to the war effort with knitting needles, bake sales, bingo games, variety shows and unflagging patriotism.

In every tangible sense the war was far away from our farm. A sprinkling of local boys enlisted, but few became casualties. Rationing, when it came in 1942, was almost meaningless: our coffee, tea, sugar and gasoline had been rationed by circumstances for a dozen years.

Emotionally, though, the war was present every waking moment in our red-white-and-blue household. In spite of all that the first obscene world war had done to him, my father was still a patriot to the depths of his soul. He was actively hating Hitler long before most of the Western world. As the Nazis gained strength in 1938 we visited Mister Adams and his radio to hear the news and bemoan the Empire's imminent peril. Once the Hitler voice ranted through the hiss and crackle of shortwave. As the news worsened in 1939 my father stomped angrily about the farm, wearing what we called his "fighting face": tight lips, pugnacious jaw, icy blue eyes glinting under the red haystacks of his frown.

A radio became essential. He bought a thirty-four-dollar mantel Philco and paid for it in two-dollar installments. On September 3 he hunched grimly over it while the broken voice of Neville Chamberlain announced that Britain was at war. For the next seven days my father was unfit to live with — scowling, glowering, calling Mackenzie King unprintable things until the latter committed Canada's support. Then he wanted to volunteer for active service. Mother soothed him out of the idea. He was far too old and frail, of course, and I was too young to manage the farm even if the army had deemed him fit for Home Guard duty, guarding prison camps.

Well, at least we had the news and its fringe benefits. Thanks to Hitler we were now in step with the golden age of radio. Now we understood all the hoary gags about Jack Benny's Maxwell car and miserly ways, Edgar Bergen's smart-ass dummy Charlie McCarthy, the weekly opening and spilling of Fibber McGee's horrendously cluttered closet, and the acerbic wit of Fred Allen and the denizens of Allen's Alley.

For us, with our hyperactive imaginations honed over years of make-believe, radio drama was sheer wonder. We never missed "Lux Radio Theatre." We wallowed in the soaps: "Pepper Young's Family," "The Guiding Light" and Oxydol's cloying old Ma Perkins. On Saturday afternoons my mother fitted her mending and sewing around the Metropolitan Opera from New York. On Saturday night my father, Larry and I set new milking records beneath the astonished Old Reddy, so we could get to the radio in time to hear Foster Hewitt's clarion call: "Hello Canada, and hockey fans in the United States and Newfoundland. . . ."

But the news had priority. Normally we monitored news at breakfast, lunch, supper and bedtime. During crises, such as the Battle of Britain, Dad came in early from the fields for extra bulletins and lived beside the radio on Sunday. We were steeped in the Hammond-organ tones of Lorne Greene, the cool urbane despatches of Edward R. Murrow and, of course, the plummy ponderous cadence of the BBC: "THIS . . . is LONDON calling . . . Now HEAH . . . is the NEWS. . . ." Once after a heavy helping of BBC, Mother complained, "The English can say less in the most time than anyone I know." My father gave her a death-ray glance and strode from the house.

We hung on Franklin Roosevelt's every ringing word, on every tingling Churchillian phrase. We huddled, shocked, around the radio in the gray Sunday twilight of December 7, 1941, as reports tumbled in from Pearl Harbor. We were elated too, for now the United States would *have* to fight and surely our side would win. It made life infinitely more bearable for my American mother who, through two years of heckling from my father, had borne single-handed the heavy burden of the U.S.A.'s nonintervention.

When the war moved to North Africa we clipped newspaper maps and marked with pins each victory and defeat. When Shamrock High School offered a weekly twenty-five-cent War Savings Stamp for students most knowledgeable in current events, the village kids discovered that the scrawny country boy who always struck out at softball had *one* skill: I steamrollered over them all to win sixteen stamps, enough for a War Savings Certificate.

We hoarded all our savings for those certificates: every one-dollar Christmas gift from Uncle Dorlan in California, every penny from gopher tails, every ten-cents-per-inch fee from the *Leader Post*. It seemed a good investment: in seven and a half years a four-dollar expenditure matured into a five-dollar certificate. Besides, as the National War Finance Committee kept reminding us, we were "doing our part."

Some impeccable authority was *always* nagging us to do our part. The Department of Munitions and Supply urged women war workers to support their warriors ("Brave Men Shall Not Die Because I Faltered," cried plucky females in *Maclean's* magazine advertisements). National Revenue assured us that "income tax is fair to all" and that the enormous wartime bite was helping preserve our "very existence." The Wartime Prices and Trade Board scared hell out of us over sugar: "You need not hoard — you must not hoard — YOU MUST OBEY THE LAW."

Bell said its telephones were working for victory; RCA said its radios were. Parker's pens were writing letters for servicemen; Kodak was taking their pictures; Coke was keeping war workers refreshed. We accepted it all, enthusiastically and without question. But how could we, out in the boondocks, measure up? How could we, O Canada, stand on guard for thee?

We saved magazines to send to servicemen. We peeled tinfoil from cigarette packages and chewing gum wrappers, salvaged old aluminum saucepans and toothpaste tubes, and gave all to the war effort. My friend Mac Smart, as head of the local chapter of the Victory Boosters Tobacco League, maintained a constant flow of nicotine to Our Boys Over There. He was a wizard at ferreting out cash for this worthy cause.

He reached a pinnacle with the great scrap iron caper of 1942. The government offered $15 for every ton of scrap turned in. Mac cycled miles through the neighborhood soliciting old ploughshares, broken harrows, discarded cook stoves and sundry other junk. Even for $7.50 cash per ton, free pickup and a chance to help beat Hitler, some neighbors declined. One said he *needed* his junk. Another snarled that servicemen could bloody well afford their own cigarettes. A third, whose religion equated smoking with original sin, would never have yielded his rusty cultivator had not Mac astutely soft-pedalled the cigarette angle and murmured vague patriotic hints of "comforts for the troops."

Then in a series of back-breaking Saturday trips, Mac and I toured the district, gut-wrenched four tons of the stuff into kindly Wally James's truck, and netted about thirty dollars for the Tobacco League. For this and other missions Mac won the honorary title of Victory Crusader. I sold the story to the *Leader Post*. The junk presumably went into tanks and battleships to defeat the Hun. And Our Boys Over There got ten thousand cigarettes, many of which — as I eventually discovered overseas myself — were briskly bartered for souvenirs and sex.

By now I was near enlistment age. We had never discussed it but I always knew I would join up and that my father would be proud. War had ended the Depression. Wheat prices soared. Coincidentally, the rains came, grasshoppers dwindled and crops grew bountiful again. I could have stayed home — essential farm workers were exempt from military service — but the thirties had left a bitter taste. In 1942 my father began managing the Shamrock lumberyard, in search of a steadier income and an easier life. For a few months after, I managed the farm while we formulated our futures.

The thought of going away was frightening. I loved my home. I was agonizingly shy. I didn't want to get shot — at least nothing more than a glamorous flesh wound. But any offspring of Jack Collins had to have patriotism oozing from his pores. And every boy in those years was seduced by the high drama of war.

Airmen were my idols. Air force recruiting posters beckoned: I could be a "WORLD TRAVELLER AT 21." Every newspaper and magazine extolled the clean-cut lads in airforce blue. We all knew about Canadian ace Buzz Beurling and his twenty-nine kills. Roy Bien joined up, and came home with the aircrew white flash in his wedge cap and the wireless air gunner's single wing on his blue chest. Girls circled him like flies around honey. I was hooked.

The prairies were dotted with airfields under the Commonwealth Air Training plan. Sometimes training craft droned through our empty sky, such a novelty that we always ran to stare. Sometimes they hedgehopped. One autumn day as I stooked in a remote coulee, a yellow Tiger Moth with the RCAF rondel skimmed over a hill, maybe two hundred feet off the ground. I had never been close to a plane before. I stood transfixed, sweaty and earthbound in my overalls and heavy boots, and my heart went out to the helmeted figure in the cockpit.

The crop of 1942 was our best ever. I slaved over the stooks. They were caught in unseasonable snow and stood out all winter, but I had built them well. In the spring the threshing machine belatedly poured a torrent of wheat and oats into our granaries. My father paid off the mortgage and other debts that had lingered for twenty-three years. Then I sent away for the RCAF brochure. When it came in the mail everyone knew what was happening. We found a renter for the farm. I hitched a ride to Moose Jaw with the ever-dependable Hugh Adams and offered my body to the recruiters.

They betrayed not one tremor of excitement over the human prize that stood before them. They looked me over indulgently and passed out sheaves of paper. When I reached the bewildering dotted pages of the color vision test, I flunked. I was blue-green color-blind, enough to rule out aircrew or any ground job involving colored lights or wiring. I asked for another color test and failed again.

"We have openings for AFMs — airframe mechanics — and cooks," said the bored recruiting officer. AFMs, he explained, handled every part of the frame-and-fabric airplanes except the engine. It seemed a logical choice for a farm boy who knew a little about woodworking, nothing about engines and thought cooking was women's work. I took mechanical aptitude tests. A corporal stared at my score and said, "You sure you don't wanta be a cook, kid?"

But at last the indifferent air force accepted me.

"Go home for the harvest, you'll be needed there," said an officer. "Right after that, report to Brandon manning pool."

At home the family joined me in condemning RCAF color vision tests. I stooked and threshed more grain and began my private goodbyes to the places I had roamed for eighteen years. With delicious melancholy I reckoned I might never come back. I scratched my name for posterity on some favorite rocks, with soft yellow writing stone. Someday, beautiful girls with heroic breasts would come upon these inscriptions, pause and exclaim . . .

*"R. J. Collins. . . . Why, that must have been Wing Commander Collins, V.C., D.F.C., D.S.O. and Bar . . . !"*

*"You don't mean . . . the one who was in all the newspapers??"*

*"Yes! The war hero! He lived here once, you know. They say he would have been a greater writer than Hemingway. But he was reported missing on his twenty-first birthday. . . ."*

Just how I would progress from airframe mechanic to air ace was a detail to be solved in later fantasies.

I rose on the final morning — after eighteen years, my last sleep ever in the farmhouse — and packed my father's worn club bag. We were all subdued. It was not just that I was going to war. The family was breaking up. Everything was breaking up. Soon the farm would be rented — this land we had loved so much, so long — and my parents and brother would move into Shamrock. Nothing would ever be the same again.

My parents' dream had come true. They were getting off the farm, seeking that easier life. Their great achievement was nearly over: they had raised a family well, in the worst of times. But now, at this last moment, we all sensed that those hard years had been the *best* years we would ever know together.

My father was wearing his fighting face. My mother performed her last loving act, the only really useful thing she could do now. She packed a huge lunch for the train trip: roast chicken, bread-and-butter sandwiches, cake, fruit. I put on my Botany Serge suit and the salt-and-pepper cloth cap that would instantly mark me as a rube upon arrival in Brandon. My dad revved the 1929 Chev and we pulled away.

When I looked back, my mother was standing on the flat stone beside the back door. It was only the second time in my life I had seen her cry.

# Epilogue

Those years have turned to sepia now, but all the people in them were, or are, real.

My father's body failed at last, although his spirit triumphed almost to the end. In 1957 he died in a Vancouver veterans' hospital — on The Coast, at last — from old age, World War I ailments and, I think, from sadness invoked by a world that no longer had a place for him or the things he believed in.

My mother at eighty-four still cooks and serves heaping meals by habit, never failing to ask, "More meat? Another piece of pie?" None of us was surprised when during her seventies she taught herself typing, learned to swim, studied conversational French, visited Expo and stayed with a French family who became her close friends. She also took a six-thousand-mile bus trip alone through North America, visiting legions of relatives, and found time to compile a book, privately printed, from the collected letters of her missionary brother.

My own brother has been a journalist for twenty-five years. Butch Gwin, Auntie May Walker, her brother Donald and most other adults of those years are dead, but Tim Adams lives, gracious as ever, in Victoria. The pretty girls with whom I was smitten did the sensible thing: married someone else. My great friend Roy Bien served with distinction in the war and returned to Saskatchewan where he still lives.

Most of my other classmates went on to be teachers, carpenters, preachers, mechanics, nurses, heads of government departments, and successful farmers. Standon still stands but is no longer a school. Shamrock survived the postwar malaise that wiped out so many small prairie towns, but its passenger train is long gone.

In 1963 I went back to my birthplace, twenty years after I slept in it for the last time. It was abandoned. Its doors flapped on broken hinges. Its shattered windows faced out blindly on the empty yard. Startled pigeons rose up with a hammer of wings as I gingerly trod the ruined living room floor. The barn and granaries and windmill were gone. The trees were half-dead, half-jungle. Quickly I turned away so the friend beside me would not see me cry.

I should have known it would be like any other deserted homestead. It was simply part of the new owner's wheat factory; he seeded and harvested grain in half-mile swoops here as on other acreages around the district.

But the house deserved better than a slow ignoble death on a lonely hill. I had a plan. I would rebuild it, restore the lawn, sink a well, cull dead and fallen timber from the tree belt but leave the birds and rabbits in peace. I would live there sometimes and other times loan it rent-free to someone who would also love and care for it. Three times I wrote the owners, offering to buy the hulk and the ten acres around it. They refused.

And now the house has vanished from the earth.

And yet . . . and yet . . . some things never die. My daughters — who, like their grandfather, can light up the world when their mood is right — sometimes sing "Brian O'Lynn."